# HELPING STUDENTS LEARN

## The Improvement of Higher Education

Harry E. Stanton
University of Tasmania

University Press of America

Library of Congress Catalog Card Number: 78-70519

*To Valerie, Peter, and Lynda*

## Acknowledgements

My greatest debt is to those who have helped me learn — my students, my teachers, and my colleagues. Special thanks are due to Bill Hall and Julie Badcock whose comments on early drafts of the book helped greatly in its final revision, and to Robyn Hill for her cheerful assistance in the typing of the manuscript.

Type set by Davies Bros Ltd, Hobart, Tasmania.

# Table of Contents

| | | |
|---|---|---|
| 1. | **Introduction** | **1** |
| 2. | **What is good teaching?** | **6** |
| | The facilitation of learning | 6 |
| | The importance of personal meaning | 7 |
| | Making learning more meaningful | 7 |
| | Relating information to student experience | 9 |
| | Increasing students' motivation to learn | 10 |
| | Reducing threat in the learning environment | 12 |
| 3. | **Who is the good teacher?** | **16** |
| | The teacher as a scholar | 16 |
| | The "competencies" of the good teacher | 17 |
| | The good teacher uses himself effectively | 19 |
| 4. | **The "best" teaching method** | **22** |
| | Identification of the best method | 22 |
| | Some difficulties with educational research | 24 |
| | Research into teaching methods — some difficulties | 25 |
| | Educational research — some findings | 27 |
| | Wide range of methods available | 29 |
| 5. | **Effective lecturing** | **34** |
| | Why lectures are criticized | 34 |
| | Strengths of the lecture method | 36 |
| | Secrets of master lecturers | 38 |
| | Structure of a lecture | 39 |
| | The development of two way communication in lectures | 41 |
| | The use of handouts | 43 |
| | The use of emphasis | 45 |
| 6. | **The productive use of small group discussion** | **47** |
| | What is a small group discussion | 47 |
| | Virtues of small group discussion | 48 |
| | Problems of small group discussion | 51 |
| | Subdividing the group | 52 |
| | Dyadic or one-to-one discussion | 53 |
| | Increasing participation of group members | 56 |
| | Improving group processes | 59 |

**7. Facilitating learning through individualized instruction**   **62**

Independence in learning    62
Personalized system of instruction (PSI)    64
Modular instruction    66
Programmed instruction    69
Individualized instruction in practical sessions    71

**8. The value of educational technology**   **74**

Systematic course design    75
The role of objectives or aims    76
The place of audio-visual media    78
The use of visuals    79
Audiotape can be helpful too    80
Using media to best effect    81
Properties and types of media    81

**9. Have we helped our students learn?**   **83**

Learning — whose responsibility    83
The evaluation of teaching    84
Why use students' evaluation    85
The pro and con of student evaluation    87
Some ways of collecting information from students    88
Why do we examine students    92
The examination system — weaknesses and improvements    95

**10. Can higher education be improved?**   **98**

Is teaching in need of improvement    98
Obstacles to change    98
Changing the teaching practices of higher education    100
Instructional Development Centres    100
Personal development of higher education teachers    105

**References**   **109**

**Index**   **115**

# Chapter I

# Introduction

This book is about "good" teaching at the tertiary level. A word can mean different things to different people, but to me, "good" means having qualities suitable to the end proposed. This is a definition drawn from Chambers Dictionary and is the one I shall be using though, no doubt, it may not be satisfactory to all readers. Perhaps that doesn't matter too much. I think most people have a reasonably similar understanding of what "good" means so that variations in individual interpretations are unlikely to invalidate the points I intend to make. These points will relate to ways in which teaching within institutions of higher education may be improved. I make no claim to comprehensiveness. Rather, I have concentrated my suggestions in those areas where my experience is greatest.

The second chapter concerns good teaching. In the light of the definition already given, I see the goal of teaching as learning. Therefore good teaching is that which facilitates learning, and is justified only insofar as it achieves this end. Similarly in chapter three, where the question of the good teacher is raised, the line taken is that he is one who helps students learn more readily than they would if left to their own devices. This viewpoint is, of course, arguable. So, too, is the claim, advanced in chapter four, that it is possible to identify good teachers. Information derived from students bulks large at this point, as it does in chapter nine where the evaluation of teaching is considered in some detail.

Chapters five, six, seven and eight concern themselves with what the good teacher does. Some of the material here, particularly that relating to course design and assessment, may seem idealistic. It isn't really. All the suggestions made stem either from personal experience or from the experience of others with whom I have worked. Everything I have suggested has worked well for somebody, somewhere. It may not work for you but until you try out some of the ideas outlined you will never know. I make no attempt to spell out a right way to teach. There is no such way. Just as there are many paths to truth, there are many ways in which to help students learn. What we all need is to be sufficiently open and flexible to sample the possibilities widely, to experiment in order to find out which particular approaches work for us. Different students and different subjects demand such flexibility, yet it is easy to fall into one teaching pattern which we retain throughout our entire academic career.

Having established a picture of the good teacher and his activities, I turn next to the thorny issue of training. Teachers in institutions of higher education, unlike their colleagues at the school level, are not required to undergo any professional preparation. The assumption operating here is that "he who knows can teach", and although this may be true, chapter ten outlines some ways in which the tertiary level teacher may be helped to improve his professional effectiveness.

As I wrote this book I continually asked myself whether it was really needed. Hadn't it all been said before? So much material is produced purely as a result of the publish or perish syndrome that one must constantly examine one's motive in adding further to the outflow from the presses. Possibly it *has* all been said before, still, the need for repetition exists. Most of us probably have enough knowledge to teach well. Unfortunately, we often fail to apply this knowledge and it is only through repetition that our consciences might be sufficiently pricked to stir us into action. If what I write can serve this purpose, generating the desire to actually try out a few of the ideas suggested, then there is some point in adding further to the already voluminous literature on higher education.

It does seem incontestable that there remains considerable room for improvement in the area of tertiary teaching. Yet, while admitting that shortcomings do exist, we must not blind ourselves to the positive achievements of higher education. An impressively large number of students have graduated from universities and colleges well equipped to cope with the professions into which they enter. Many of these think of their higher education days with pleasure, remembering much of value including teachers, courses that stimulated interest in areas which became lifetime concerns, and mind expanding discussion with peers. There is much of great worth in higher education despite its weaknesses.

However, if improvement is to be effected, it seems necessary to consider these weaknesses. Saunders (1968), writing from the viewpoint of a student, outlines several criticisms of the education provided at institutions of higher learning. The first of these is that academic staff do not seem to view their teaching role as a vital one. Ability as a teacher seems to carry with it no rewards in terms of improved appointment or promotion prospects. It is research work, measured normally by the yardstick of publication record, which earns the prizes. There would be no real objection to this state of affairs if a strong correlation between research ability and teaching excellence could be demonstrated. Despite the vehemence of academic opinion affirming the existence of such a link, empirical evidence has, so far, failed to offer any support.

Hammond, Meyer and Miller (1969), consider that the best and only data in the area has been provided by Voeks (1962) and Bresler (1968), both of whom concluded that teaching quality and research quality were largely unrelated. Flood Page (1972) too, in his review of the literature pertaining to this area, could find no scientific evidence supporting the proposition, so often heard in the realms of higher education, that a man cannot be a good teacher unless he is also a skilled and active researcher. Such findings continue to be ignored. Belief in the existence of a significant and valid link between teaching and research is as strong as ever, producing unfortunate results in terms of the poor quality of instruction to which Saunders objects. Perhaps Caplow and McGee (1961), do overstate the case when they maintain:

"Although in most occupations men are judged by how well they perform their normal duties, the academic man is judged almost exclusively by his performance in a kind of part-time voluntary job which he creates for himself . . . It is only a slight exaggeration to say that academic success is likely to come to the man who has learned to neglect his assigned duties in order to have more time and energy to pursue his private professional interests". (p.327).

Exaggeration or not, there is a germ of truth in this statement which goes far towards explaining why teaching at the tertiary level is undervalued.

It is difficult, however, to blame academics for doing those things for which they are rewarded. This is, after all, a basic principle of learning. We continue to behave in ways which produce pleasant consequences and desist from behaviour which goes unrewarded. The operation of this principle ensures that the ambitious academic must give precedence to research and publication, for therein lies the way to advancement.

In terms of the university reward structure, it is more sensible to produce a book which may be of little interest to anyone outside of a handful of fellow academics than it is to spend a lot of time designing courses, experimenting with different teaching methods, and listening to students' problems.

It is a matter of regret to those of us interested in improving the learning environment within institutions of higher education that so little of this research effort is directed towards the teaching activities of academic staff. Attempts to investigate aspects of teaching and learning within tertiary institutions are minimal compared to discipline-oriented research. Flood-Page (1972) is trenchant in his criticism of this attitude, pointing out that university and college teachers rarely display the attitudes they preach to others — reasonableness, dispassionate weighing of evidence, and rational argument — when their own activities are being considered. Continuing, he says:

> "We university teachers spend much of our time praising the research method and using it on every subject in the universe except ourselves. If we wish universities to justify and sustain the position in the world which they claim today, we must have the courage and humility to practice on ourselves what we so emphatically preach to others". (p 117).

This very human weakness of avoiding investigation into our own teaching activities provides substance for Saunders' second criticism, that universities and colleges permit traditional methods of instruction to prevail without due consideration of alternatives which may be more effective in promoting learning. That such a situation does exist is hard to deny, though it is explicable in the light of the previously described university reward system. The development of new teaching techniques is often something of a part-time occupation while lecturers direct their main energies elsewhere. It must also be realised that academic staff are quite often unaware of variants from the traditional method of lecturing. They experience none of the pre-service training considered mandatory for school teachers nor, as a rule, do they receive very much help of an in-service nature. Although the provision of staff development centres is an attempt to remedy this omission, many of the lecturers most in need of assistance do not avail themselves of the service. Again, this is probably a matter of time allocation. Attendance at a training course may not seem the most rewarding way to use the time that is available, for there are no institutional rewards for such behaviour.

Lacking a knowledge of the range of methods available, academics tend to teach in the same way they themselves were taught. Rather uncritically, they drop into the traditional pattern of their discipline, assuming the way to provide learning experiences is to *tell* students. This is usually accomplished by means of a 50-minute, uninterrupted monologue during which students are expected to note all the important information. The assumption operating here, usually unstated and unrealised, is that because the lecturer was able to learn in this way, his own students should be able to do likewise.

What is overlooked by such reasoning is that a university lecturer is the product of a long selection process. He gains his appointment because he has demonstrated his ability as a learner, coping with the lecture-examination system successfully. However, he is not an average student; he is exceptional. Yet, when he becomes a lecturer, which position he achieves by demonstrating that he has been taught rather than by demonstrating that he can teach, he often overlooks that he was exceptional, setting quite inappropriate standards for his students. When they fail to measure up to such expectations, they are given more of the same — more information in lectures, longer book lists, more tests. Unwilling or unable to vary his teaching approach, such a lecturer is locked into a pattern, becoming the stereotype at whom Saunders' criticism is aimed. What he is doing is trying to produce his own kind, conditioning them in turn to teach as they were taught.

The fault is not necessarily only that of the individual lecturer. As Rowntree (1974) has pointed out, the mileu in which he has his being makes it easy for him to behave in this manner:

"Education has always played its cards 'close to the chest'. It abounds with vague and unstated goals, implicit acceptance of constraints, hidden assumptions about students, private teacher-student transactions in closed classrooms, secret modes and unexplained rationales of assessment and grading of students, and an equivocal attitude to institutional self-improvement. Much of the thinking and feeling that goes into education may be good and honourable, much may be not; but the vast majority of it never gets debated . . . except at the most superficial level. And it is difficult to be vigilant about what is hidden from view". (p 10-11).

The absence of discussion about teaching methods to which Rowntree draws attention militates against change. Past attitudes persist because new lecturers are rarely given the opportunity to discuss ideas about their teaching. Not that it is always this bad. Ferguson (1975), writing about the Open University, makes it clear that one of the biggest advantages his institution enjoys is its exposed position. All over the world, academics, students and members of the general public may read, watch, and listen to Open University material. Such scrutiny ensures that great care is taken over the quality of teaching. No course sees the light of day without long hours of discussions, testing and analysis. However, Ferguson himself realises that such time investment in teaching is not the norm.

A point made by Rowntree, which is also implicit in Ferguson's comments, concerns clarity of aims. So often students don't know what is expected of them. This is, in fact, Saunders' third and final criticism of the teaching to which he was exposed. Faced with overloaded syllabi and with lecturers anxious to cover the course, students were frequently so immersed in vast quantities of material that they had no time for understanding. Aronson (1972), in his preface to *The Social Animal,* puts this rather wittily: "Students, in effect, ask us what time it is, and we present them with a chart showing the various time zones around the world, a history of time-telling from the sun dial to the Bulova Accutron, and a detailed description of the anatomy of the wrist-watch."

The wood is so well concealed by the trees that it is often difficult for students to understand why they are studying certain material. What is its purpose? What is it supposed to achieve? What are they expected to do with it? Within the Australian context, Little (1970) has commented that low student motivation is usually a reaction to the ambivalent, cloudy and sometimes negative expectations transmitted by teachers. He is not alone in this belief, for many critics of higher education stress aimlessness as the most important single cause of ineffective teaching.

Aimlessness in this sense refers to actual courses. Students are often left uncertain of what they are expected to do in order to satisfy their lecturer they are worthy of a pass. When the objectives of a course are unclear, a great deal of unnecessary anxiety is generated. Uncertainty has this effect on us all. We can easily become paralysed, unable to take action, because we simply don't know what is expected of us. A different sort of uncertainty, just as damaging, is pointed out by Van der Berghe

4

(1970) in his satiric book, *Academic gamesmanship.* He outlines the situation in which lecturers exhort their students to think for themselves, something they have been conditioned not to do since their infancy. This comes as something of a shock but the students soon realise that most of their instructors don't really expect them to carry their independence of mind to the lengths of disagreeing with their mentors. This relieves the pressure until one or two lecturers actually penalise students for uncritical agreement with what they are told. "So", as Van der Berghe put it, "the poor student never quite knows where he stands, a situation which, among laboratory rats, leads to experimental neurosis." (p 26).

Each of the three criticisms discussed, underevaluation of the teaching role, inflexibility of instructional methods, and aimlessness, have been made against institutions of higher education many times by many people. Other shortcomings, too, are often mentioned, but these three seem to stand out as a combined Achilles heel. Yet, to play the part of critic is easy. No great intellectual brilliance is necessary to point out deficiencies in the institutions within which we work. The difficult achievement is to suggest ways in which these deficiencies may be reduced, leading to a general strengthening of the institution concerned.

Hopefully, the suggestions contained in this book may provide some guidance to lecturers, helping them to meet the criticisms of poor teaching methodology, inflexibility and aimlessness which have been outlined above. Indirectly, through the discussion of practical aspects of higher education, they may also play some small part in encouraging academic staff to view their teaching role more positively.

Perhaps I could be accused of setting up a straw man in this introduction. The picture I've painted may be totally biased, and the deficiencies outlined only apparent in a small minority of institutions. All may be well in academe. I really don't believe this is so. Fred Emery is reputed to have said: "In secondary school, they poke your eyes out . . .In universities they teach you braille," If this book can do nothing else, it may help us teach braille more effectively.

# Chapter 2

# What is good teaching?

## The Facilitation of Learning

Teaching is the facilitation of learning. It is warranted to the extent that it makes learning easier and/or more efficient than it would otherwise be. If, through his exposure to a teacher, a student learns something better than he would have done alone, such teaching is justified. This is a personal view and one with which many would not agree. I take the line that if a student has not learnt, then a lecturer has not taught. An alternative view, and one which is more popular, is that teaching consists of certain acts performed by a lecturer. Whether a student learns as a result of these acts is largely immaterial, for the lecturer has fulfilled his function. This function is normally seen in terms of transmitting information. If a lecturer gathers information and makes it available to his students then he is teaching. The method most commonly used to achieve this purpose is the lecture, a talking-listening strategy which has endured for many years.

Use of the formal lecture as the main vehicle of teaching in higher education is a result of certain false assumptions about the nature of learning. It is assumed that giving students knowledge and information through "telling" is an effective method of helping them learn such material. Acceptance of such a view entails the belief that education is primarily a process of accumulating information which is then stored for use on later, appropriate occasions. Several decades of research on learning have made little impact in changing this view despite the evidence produced (eg Milton, 1973) that it is incorrect. By our adherence to the talking-listening method of the lecture, we share the delusion referred to by John Holt (1967):

"We teachers . . . are in the grip of an astonishing delusion. We think that we can take a picture, a structure, a working model of something constructed in our minds out of long experience and familiarity, and by turning that model into a string of words transplant it whole into the mind of someone else" (p 178).

I am not necessarily suggesting that lectures are bad per se. As will be indicated later, there are many occasions upon which they serve a very valuable purpose. What I am suggesting is that the particular concept of how people learn which is implicit in their use is one which stands in urgent need of revision. This is no new thought. Learning theorists and educationalists have for years been arguing against the view of the learner as essentially passive, simply there to receive information poured in by a teacher. Much lip service is paid to this alternative view, yet the behaviour of most academic staff would indicate that it has made no real impression upon them. Intellectually they may accept that students should be given more responsibility for their own learning, more freedom to explore areas that interest them, but such cognitions do not prevent them continuing to act in a more traditional way. Their behaviour implies acceptance of the belief that their task is to transmit information to passive students who then demonstrate their "learning" by feeding back this material in the form of examination answers. Such an approach, I would argue, does not really help the student learn. Therefore, as I have previously defined good teaching in terms of the facilitation of learning, I would argue that this information transmitting strategy is unworthy of that accolade. It is not, however, a complete failure, for it does go part of the way towards the creation of a favorable learning environment. What is lacking is a further ingredient to involve the learner as an active participant instead of a passive recipient.

## The Importance of Personal Meaning

Such an ingredient has been provided by Combs, Avila & Purkey (1971) in a three phase model of the teaching process. The first two phases, gathering information and making it available to students, have already been mentioned. It is the third which is so important, that of helping students to discover the personal meaning of information so they behave differently as a result of teaching. To Combs, Avila & Purkey, this provides the definition of learning.

"Learning is the discovery of meaning. The problem of learning . . . always involves two aspects. One is the acquisition of new knowledge or experience; the other has to do with the individiual's discovery of the meaning of information for him. The provision of information can be controlled by an outsider, with or without the co-operation of the learner . . . The discovery of meaning, however, can only take place in people and cannot occur without the involvement of persons" (1971, p 91).

Herein lies the rationale for my definition of teaching as the facilitation of learning. Unless we can help our students discover personal meaning in the information we make available to them, we can hardly be said to be teaching.

Yet we find it so easy to stop before we reach this third phase. Telling students what they need to know and having them tell it back to us, often in our own words, imposes little strain. If students haven't learned, as reflected in their examination papers, it is their fault. It is easy to say: "Well, I gave them the information. It's up to them. If they don't learn it, it is their funeral." Unfortunately, it so often is. Students' examination failure can thus be seen as entirely their own faults. No blame can be attached to the lecturer. After all, he did dispense the information.

Maybe this is true. Perhaps it is always the fault of the student. However, acceptance of Combs' viewpoint would suggest that the lecturer, too, has some responsibility. Obviously he cannot do a student's learning for him, but he can offer help and guidance along the way. If teaching doesn't facilitate learning in this way, by providing such help and guidance, what use is it? Better to leave the student to his own devices and reduce the enormous expenditure on higher education. Yet, once we admit that teaching should provide a facilitative learning environment, we, as teachers, must accept some share of responsibility for our students' success or failure. If they perform poorly, it is not all their fault. Neither is it all our fault. Lecturers and students are engaged in a co-operative enterprise with successful learning as the goal. As teachers, it is our task to facilitate this process, not so much by providing information, though this is important, but by helping students discover its meaning. In the *Prophet,* Gilbran (1926), when speaking of the teacher, put it so beautifully:

"If he is indeed wise he does not bid you enter the house of his wisdom but rather leads you to the threshold of your own mind."

## Making Learning More Meaningful

This is no easy task. If we accept that learning has two components, information and meaning, and that our more difficult task lies with the latter, we are faced with a problem. How can we help students to make sense of the material with which they are faced? Continuance of a teaching strategy in which there is a constant outpouring of information by means of lectures is unlikely to provide an answer. Most of us have far more information than we need. Our problem is to apply and use what we have. This takes time, for the development of understanding, which is a necessary precursor to effective use of knowledge, cannot be rushed. It cannot be measured very accurately either and we are often uncertain whether our students have understood the material with which they are working. Holt (1960) has suggested he feels he understands something if and when he can do at least some of these things; state it in his own words; give examples of it; recognise it in various guises and circumstances; see connections between it and other facts and ideas; make use of it in various ways; foresee some of its consequences; and state its opposite or converse. The time consuming nature of the process is clearly evident in such a list of criteria.

One approach, then, to facilitating students' learning is to reduce the amount of information we present to them. Concentration on relatively few concepts and principles rather than many facts is likely to increase students' understanding by giving them more time to explore the material for personal meaning. This may not be easy to do, of course. Deeply ingrained within us is the tremendous importance of the course we teach and the vital nature of every piece of information we include. Quite genuinely we feel that students would be greatly deprived if even one sub-section of a particular topic was omitted. Yet I wonder how realistic is this approach. The content of any course is only one possible sample of the material available. Other lecturers are likely to include a quite different sample under the same course title. Often material, quite irrelevant to present student needs, is transmitted, the rationale being that "if they don't need it now, they will one of these days." However, when one of these days arrives the information is not remembered because, at the time of its presentation, it was meaningless.

Most courses would profit from severe pruning. Recently I was speaking with a lecturer, I'll call him John Custer, who was complaining of his difficulty in fitting some new material into his course. I asked him what he intended to eliminate in order to make room for it. The idea of deleting material simply hadn't occurred to him. For years he had been continually adding new information while retaining all his original material too. The result was a mad gallop through a series of crammed lectures with no time available for students to digest what was being presented. Unable to see the wood for the trees, they were reduced to rote memorization, a most unsatisfactory method if understanding is the goal. When John did critically examine his course, he found several topics that could be eliminated without serious loss, thus he made room for the new material. It seems obvious that we should practice such a technique of replacement, of updating, rather than simply adding more and more information till students simply give up any attempt to make sense of it. If we proceed in this fashion, continually adding to courses, we are certainly doing little to help students derive meaning from their studies.

Reducing the informational content of a course to allow a more leisurely pace carries an additional benefit. Lectures are likely to be better. This point will be elaborated upon in a later chapter, but experience suggests that the most effective lecturers are those who attempt to cover no more than three or four key points. This permits time for illustration, example, and discussion in which students can take part. Too often we assume that the small group is the only place for discussion. It isn't. Lectures may also be used to provide opportunities for students to identify errors and

8

gain additional information from peers and lecturer where needed. The meaningfulness of instructional material is increased by allowing the learner to indicate what gaps exist for him at the time they appear, and then filling these gaps with correct information. Usually the time such gaps appear is in lectures and this is the time to deal with them, not at a tutorial several days later. Such learning opportunities disappear when a lecturer is so anxious to "cover the ground" that he pours out vast quantities of material irrespective of whether students understand it or not. This is not facilitating learning. It is not good teaching.

Returning to John Custer whom I mentioned earlier, let us assume that he has organized his course in such a way that students are given time to think about and discuss the reduced amount of information he presents. There are certain actions he may now take to increase the meaningfulness of this material.

## Relating Information to Student Experience

Firstly, learning is more likely to occur if new information is related to the student's experience. The old teaching bromide of working from the known to the unknown embraces this idea. Snygg (1972) has pointed out that no matter how well it is expressed, a concept can only be accepted if it fits into the student's own cognitive field. If this doesn't occur, because the concept is too alien to his previous experience, the student is likely to regard it as a statement of fact which has no relevance to his real life. Snygg suggests that most lecture and reading material is disposed of in this way. The result is that the information is likely to be unavailable when required at a later date because, at the time of its transmission, it had no personal meaning for the student. It was difficult for him to file it in his mind because there were no appropriate anchoring concepts to which it could be attached.

One way of overcoming this difficulty may be to use advance organizers. (Ausubel, 1968). These are concepts and principles introduced before the main part of the instructional material. Their function is to explain and organize this material, linking it to the student's previous experience. This helps the student find some meaning to the new information and hopefully makes it easier to learn, avoiding the necessity of rote memorization.

Another way in which a lecturer may prepare his students for new material is to turn the headings and sub-headings of his lecture into questions, discussing these briefly before commencing his presentation. At this time, students' previous experience should be tapped through questioning and then related to the new material which is to come. They are then more likely to listen attentively to the lecture which is to provide answers to the questions posed, for they have already discovered that their previous experience is unequal to this task. The same technique is also useful when a reading assignment is set, with headings being turned into questions.

There are other teaching principles that are relevant in this context. Although tertiary level students are expected to reason abstractly, it is often helpful to provide concrete examples as a starting point. These might include case studies, practical problems, audio-visual materials and specimens. This is, in fact, the basis of inductive teaching where students are encouraged to draw their own conclusions from specific examples. Such generalizing is encouraged by a "sandwich" method of presentation. Concrete material is used as a starting point, then the particular abstraction is taught, and finally students apply it to further concrete situations and new examples. Without the use of realia or audio-visual substitutes, inductive teaching is severely handicapped and learning made more difficult. As we grow older, for most of us, our reliance on the concrete diminishes (Piaget & Inhelder, 1969), but this does not imply that we can do without it altogether. The application of pure reason may be great, but we are more likely to facilitate successfully the learning of our students by using practical examples to arrive at this state.

Just as working from the known to the unknown, and from the concrete to the abstract have been enshrined as effective learning principles for many years, so too has that of proceeding from the whole to the part. This approach finds its rationale in Gestalt psychology which would claim that the whole is more than the sum of its parts. When we learn something one step at a time without seeing the overall pattern into which each fits, we have little opportunity to perceive the significance of what we are doing. However, once we can visualize the larger framework, the individual parts take on meaning of their own. We can see their purpose, their importance, and so our learning is made easier. Instead of memorizing a number of apparently isolated facts we can understand how they hang together in a coherent whole, and our learning becomes meaningful.

This principle is embodied in the teaching technique of backward chaining, or mathetics, first introduced by Gilbert (1962). This approach is applicable where the learning of sequences is involved, its key concept being that of teaching the final step in the chain first. Rowntree (1974) uses the teaching of scientific problem solving as an example of how this might be done. The steps involved, in their usual order of presentation, would be:

A. Recognize and state a problem.
B. Form a hypothesis.
C. Devise a test of the hypothesis.
D. Carry out the test.
E. Interpret the results of the test.

Gilbert's procedure is to reverse this order. He would present to the students' data on steps A to D for a particular problem and then demonstrate how to do the interpretation. Another problem would then be considered, this time the students receiving data on steps A to C and being asked to carry out the test and interpret the results. Next, A and B would be given for a new problem with the students required to devise a test, carry it out and interpret the results. With the next problem, only A would be presented. Students would be expected to carry out steps B to E themselves. Finally, when faced with a problem, students would go through all five steps by themselves. Such a procedure has the great advantage of immediately acquainting the learner with the final product. He then sees how this end result is achieved, completing the entire sequence several times while he does so. This is helpful to the student in that the relevance of each step is apparent. There is a clearly discernible meaning in all he does. Each time a sequence is "run", the lecturer should teach a new step, remind the student of the last step he learned, and then expect him to finish the chain unaided.

Procedures such as those already outlined help students find increased meaning in their courses. As this occurs, their motivation increases. Like learning, motivation may be defined in a variety of ways, but I use the word here to mean a student's desire to engage in learning. Creation of a learning environment in which this desire may be increased is now considered.

## Increasing Students Motivation to Learn.

Rowntree (1974) has identified several key motivational issues when he comments: "The student is motivated when he identifies with the objectives to which the learning leads . . . Problems with motivation really arise only when we try to teach people things they don't want to know; then there is the temptation to rely on negative reinforcers like fear of failure or punishment." (p.114).

Students will learn what they want to learn and will have great difficulty in learning material in which they are not interested. Motivation is often seen in terms of a fancy wrapping on the instructional package which will hopefully convince the student that it is worth learning. But this approach is of little value if the learner cannot feel anything about the contents of the package, for we then find ourselves in the position of throwing answers like stones at the heads of those who haven't asked the questions. (Brown, 1971). The problem is to involve students in the goals which are set for them so that they feel a desire to attain them. Feel is an important word in this context, for it would appear that learning is most effective when it operates on both an emotional and a cognitive level.

Duberman (1968), writing of his experimental seminars in philosophy, has stressed the need to make such sessions more than an intellectual exchange. Opinions and values, he argues, are more likely to be revealed when the atmosphere encourages, rather than suppresses, emotional interaction. Opinions are never shaped solely by reasoning, but are always influenced by emotionally charged personal relationships and encounters. Since students' beliefs have been formed in a multi-dimensional setting, it seems unreasonable to expect a re-examination of such beliefs in a one-dimensional setting in which intellect is everything. Herein lies much of the value of the small discussion group which permits a relatively free exchange of views. Where emotional problems surface in such a setting, they can be dealt with, thereby contributing to group cohesiveness. To a lesser extent, hostilities, feelings of failure and rejection, and anxieties about the learning situation may also be handled in lectures if teachers are able to let go of their obsessive need to cover the ground. Opportunities for contact outside the classroom can often prove very valuable in this respect, allowing lecturer and student to relate as human beings rather than as players of professional roles. Actually, such informal contacts were identified by Gaff (1973) as the distinguishing characteristic of a faculty which exerted an influence on its students as opposed to one which had no such influence. These points will be discussed more fully in later chapters, but it does seem reasonable to suggest that one way of increasing motivation is to provide opportunities for students to express their feelings about the material with which they are faced.

This is particularly true if students are given an opportunity to contribute to goal setting at the commencement of a new course. A student needs to have knowledge of the goals set for him, of what is required of him, if he is to learn, but his involvement will be much greater if he feels he has had some share in shaping these objectives. This may be done during the first course meeting when the lecturer can outline; firstly his objectives and the reasons why he considers them to be important; secondly, the teaching methods he intends to use; and thirdly, the way in which he intends to assess whether students have been successful in attaining the objectives. Students are then invited to express their opinions and feelings about this "blueprint", suggesting modifications where appropriate. Of course, these must be justified. Such a procedure enables both lecturer and students to gain an overview of the course and to examine its rationale. The "relevance" of objectives can be argued, the suitability of the teaching methods examined, and the appropriateness of assessment techniques questioned. Often no real change results from such discussions. Sometimes, quite serious flaws are revealed and changes are necessary. However, irrespective of the outcome, students are involved, at least to some extent, in the course planning. They are given the opportunity to express their feelings about it and to institute changes if these can be justified. This assists them to identify with the course objectives and, hopefully, to develop some desire to achieve them. Although it is true that students prefer to learn about things which interest them, this is not to say that we must stop with these pre-existing motives. Often, if we can be open and flexible about our objectives and course, we can create new motives, perhaps rousing in students a desire to learn the new content. I think this usually becomes possible only when the learner is involved in contributing to the important decisions about his learning. His contributions need not stop after this initial session. Half way through the course, for example, lecturer and students may suspend formal classes and discuss what has been taught, what has been learned and how learning might be improved in the rest of the course. Such open interchange not only improves motivation; it also facilitates learning.

Students in institutions of higher education are not children. They are capable of taking considerable responsibility for their own learning if they are allowed to do so. Whether we do permit such freedom is really a matter of our view of man. Either we see the need to control our students because of our belief that they have to be made to behave, or we believe they are born with the ability to find their own way and to make their own discoveries. These views are at opposite poles of a continuum and the most appropriate position is possibly somewhere between the two. For many years, imbued with the ideals of Carl Rogers (1969) I attempted to establish a learning environment in which my students were given "freedom to learn" (Stanton, 1975a). Perhaps I moved too far towards the uncontrolled end of the continuum for, on sober reflection, (Stanton, 1975b), I realized many students required a more structured learning situation. Yet, within most tertiary institutions, I think we err too much in the other direction, depriving students of opportunities to discover things for themselves. Too frequently we present learners with the results of inquiry instead of helping them recreate the process of inquiry. Howe (1967) puts it neatly when he says: "I think teaching too often concentrates on showing students the way before it has wakened in them the least desire to go there." (p.264). This is the basic motivational issue, awakening a desire for learning and then helping students satisfy this desire. Involving them in course planning is one way of so doing.

Reducing threat is another. Snygg (1972) argues that normal course material is so irrelevant to the learner's needs that it is ignored. To prevent this happening, the lecturer uses the threat of failure and humiliation in an effort to force the student to learn. Such behaviour is unlikely to develop a facilitative learning atmosphere. If learning is a function of an individual's exploration and discovery of meaning (Combs et.al. 1974), such learning is unlikely to occur when we feel threatened. Firstly, most of us develop "tunnel vision" under such conditions, narrowing our range of perception until we are aware of only that which threatens us. Such limited perception interferes with learning. Secondly, under threat, we normally defend our existing position even more vehemently. Again, this attitude is prejudicial to learning for it works against us modifying our existing cognitive structure. To promote learning, then, it would seem necessary to reduce or eliminate threat and it is to a consideration of how this might be done that we now turn.

*Reducing Threat in the Learning Environment*

Combs, Avila & Purkey (1971) crystallize the essential issue here when they say:

"To a very large extent, creating the proper atmosphere for learning is a matter of dealing with challenge and threat . . . people feel challenged when they are confronted with problems that interest them and which seem to lie within their capacities of solution. People feel threatened, on the other hand, when they are confronted with problems they do not feel able to deal with." (p.222).

When considered in this light, our use of competition as a motivation technique is highly suspect. For those students who feel they have a chance of winning, competition has a motivating effect. However, when learners who do not believe they have much chance of success are forced to compete for marks and grades, they do not find the experience motivating. Instead, it is very threatening. Yet, while discouraging co-operative enterprises, we continue to set up situations in which students compete with each other. Peer teaching and group evaluation, for example, play no major role in higher education institutions, yet students can often teach each other very effectively, creating a very enjoyable learning atmosphere while they do so. Greater use of such co-operative environments would be one way of reducing threat.

Another approach is to encourage experimentation, flexibility and openness on the part of students. A lecturer can do this by modelling such qualities in his own behaviour and reinforcing them when they appear in his students. Acceptance of the value of such attributes will mean letting go of the idea that mistakes are sinful. Much of our learning is through our mistakes for, as human beings, we are far from perfect and are constantly making errors. Tolerance for mistakes, giving up the assumption that knowledge is fixed and certain, and avoidance of slavish devotion to authority will all help the lecturer create a relatively threat-free environment. However, if we cling to the belief that there is only one best way of solving a problem, one which has already been discovered by the "experts", we inhibit learning. Many of our students have already been conditioned to believe that they should not trust themselves, their own feelings and judgements. Instead they are encouraged to accept the pronouncements of others who have the right answers. Implied in such education is that the learner cannot contribute anything of value. It has already been done and his task is to learn it. Such a view puts pressure on a student who is forced into the position of denying the evidence of his own senses. His feeling of self-worth is diminished and his individuality threatened. The outcome is the person who doesn't know if a painting or piece of music is good until he is told by an "expert". This is not to deny that experts can provide valuable knowledge, only to affirm the right of the student to learn some things for himself in an atmosphere supportive of his efforts.

Students may be supported in other ways too. Offering assistance with study methods helps them cope more successfully with course material and so reduces the threat posed by the learning environment. In particular, virtually all tertiary level students spend long hours reading text books and journals, often with very little result in terms of knowledge gained. Faced with the necessity of such reading and aware of their inability to extract the required material, students feel a sense of mounting pressure. Every additional assignment can add to this feeling until the whole learning environment becomes one of threat and stress. Although most institutions of higher education do have student counsellors to offer assistance in this area, lecturing staff are not precluded from also making a contribution.

Perhaps all that is necessary on many occasions is to explain to students that there exists various, well-tried techniques of increasing reading efficiency and showing them how they might be used. One of the most successful of these is the SQ3R method (Robinson, 1946). This involves:

Survey — Glance over the book's table of contents, preface, introduction, chapter headings, sub-headings and summaries in order to find out what major ideas are presented and their sequence. This overview should be done quickly.

Question — Turn chapter headings and sub-headings into questions, or formulate other specific questions to which answers must be sought. This generates a seeking attitude to the material.

Read — Read the material in order to find answers to the questions posed. This approach makes reading more purposeful, preventing the aimless, undirected work which so often characterizes study behaviour.

Recite — Look away from the book and briefly recite the answers to the questions. This may be done verbally, or by writing down cue phrases from memory. Only outline notes are required at this stage, no copying being done.

Review — Once the chapter has been completed, look over the notes to get a bird's-eye view of the ideas raised and their relationships to each other. A check on memory should be made through a further recitation of key points.

For every *section* of the chapter, questions should be formulated, answers found through reading, and some form of recitation carried out. Although this may sound a very time consuming approach, the whole SQ3R process takes very little longer than the single careful reading which is the more usual study technique. The gains in improved learning make this little extra time an excellent investment on the part of the student.

Another equally sound method of studying written material is RSVP. (Staton, 1966). This system embraces four steps:

Review:- the material which has preceded the present assignment; then
Study:- the present assignment by reading it carefully; then
Verbalize:- it in your own words; then
Preview:- the material which is coming next.

This is a general study method which, although it does apply to text book reading, is also very suitable for deriving maximum benefit for lectures. As a student waits for a lecture to begin, he quickly reviews his notes, refreshing his memory on material covered previously. During the lecture, he listens carefully, noting the key ideas and when it has finished, he tries to express these in his own words, verbally and in writing. Later, he turns to his text, reading the material which is to come, knowing that the next lecture will be easier to understand if he has previously sensitized himself to its content. As with SQ3R, this RSVP technique improves student learning without any real increase in amount of study time.

So too does the use of self-reward. When a person, be he lecturer or student, behaves the way he desires, he should immediately reward himself. In a learning situation, this may mean that the student listens to ten minutes of music as a reward for fifty minutes study. If music is not particularly reinforcing, perhaps a cup of coffee, a telephone call to a friend, or a walk around the block may better serve the purpose. The actual reward used doesn't matter so long as it is something the individual likes doing. Because of this pleasant consequence, study behaviour is encouraged. Similarly, where two tasks need to be done, the more pleasant one may serve as a reward for the other. Therefore, it is preferable to complete the less desirable task first, an embodiment of grandmother's wisdom that the vegetables are to be eaten before the ice cream appears.

The techniques outlined above can help students improve the efficiency of their study, and they are only three among many. Additional methods may be found in Maddox (1963), Mace (1932) Robinson (1946), and Rowntree (1970). By making such information available to their students, lecturers help reduce the threat of the environment. In so doing, they are "facilitating learning". This is "good teaching" for, as has been made plain throughout this chapter, I regard the two terms as synonymous. If a lecturer helps his students to learn, I would suggest he is teaching well.

# Chapter 3

# Who is the good teacher?

In the previous chapter, I suggested that good teaching is the facilitation of learning. Similarly, in answering the question posed by this chapter heading, I would maintain that the good teacher is one who helps his students learn. Perhaps this could be stated even more strongly. If a lecture does not facilitate student learning, can he be called a teacher at all? We would not, for instance, call a man a salesman if no-one bought the goods he was trying to sell. This may be an invidious comparison but it seems a reasonable one. Although I can understand the self-protective instinct which leads us to maintain that a man can be called a teacher, even a good teacher, whether his students learn from him or not, I cannot accept it as a rational statement. Not everyone would share my view, for there are certain definitions of good teaching which embody the irrationality to which I refer.

## The Teacher as a Scholar

One of these is that the good scholar is the good teacher. Based on the rationale that he who knows can teach others, this definition has enjoyed a long life. It is still, perhaps, the most widely held view at the tertiary level. I would not want to deny that some good scholars are good teachers. What I would wish to question, though, is the insistence that the two qualities necessarily go together. As pointed out in the first chapter, what empirical evidence we do possess on this question would indicate that scholarship, defined in terms of publications and research, and teaching ability are independent variables. They may be found together in the same person or they may not. Therefore, to identify a man as a good scholar, and then use this criteria as the measure of his teaching ability does not appear to be sound reasoning. Yet, this is the way in which tertiary level appointments are normally made. It reminds me of a little story related by Shannon (1971) about the way pigs used to be weighed in Vermont. In his words:

"We'd put a board across a fence, balancing the board at right angles to the fence. After placing the pig on one end of the board, we stacked rocks on the other end until the pigs and the rocks seemed to strike a balance. Then we'd guess how much the rocks weighed, and that became the accurate weight of the pig." (p 81).

This may be too harsh a judgement but others have been even harsher in suggesting that scholarship is *negatively* correlated with teaching ability. A. S. Neill of Summerhill fame is quoted as saying that good mathematicians are the last people capable of teaching mathematics, and Flood-Page (1970) has argued that this principle has general applicability. He maintains that a good scholar who has done extremely well under traditional university methods is likely to be in a different universe from the majority of students and is quite unable to understand the difficulties which it is the object of a good teacher to remove. I feel this argument does have some merit, but to generalize that all good scholars make poor teachers is as unwarranted as the opposite assumption which I have criticized earlier. Great teachers do not appear to be remembered for their scholarship. As Goode (1964) has pointed out, although a man's academic achievements may cause him to be recognized as a scholar, it is "something else" which will give him a high place as a teacher. This "something else" has often been defined in terms of particular competencies possessed by teachers.

## The "Competencies" of the Good Teacher

The underlying assumption of this approach is: "If we know what the expert teachers do, or are like, we can teach the beginner to be like that." (Combs et.al, 1974. p2). Decades of research generated by this assumption have usually resulted in lists of competencies which presumably characterize the good teacher. These lists often grow to inordinate length because much human behaviour is situation specific and varies according to the particular circumstances prevailing at the time of action. This creates a very depressing situation for the beginning teacher who is faced with an ideal of excellence to which he cannot hope to aspire. Yet, apparently this is what is expected of him. For example, a conference on "Superior Teachers" (Combs, 1964) produced a description involving twenty desirable characteristics which included such items as: "Understanding the process of becoming," "possessing humility," "acting with integrity," and "believing in God."

Actually, many longer lists do exist, all proposing an ideal creation which has no parallel in reality. Most of these catalogues of desired competencies are designed by educationalists, but students, too, have produced comparable lists of attributes as they respond to the inquiries of researchers. Gadzella (1968), for example, has developed a 25-item questionnaire entitled Student Views of an 'Ideal' Professor which she has used with American students to identify the characteristics of successful and unsuccessful lecturers. Replications have been carried out in Canada (Meuller, Roach & Malone, 1971) and in Australia (Stanton, 1972a) which indicate a general uniformity among students as to the attributes they consider desirable in those who teach them. The 'ideal' lecturer in a university or college should: (i) have a thorough knowledge of his subject; (ii) be enthusiastic about and interested in the material he teaches; (iii) be capable of inspiring the students he teaches, and (iv) be able to communicate with students on a level they can comprehend. This brief list seems more reasonable and attainable, suggesting perhaps that competencies seen as important by students may be a better guide than those provided by educational theorists.

Some support for this view may be derived from Sheffield's (1974) study of effective teaching in Canadian universities. The assumption underlying his investigation was that the most appropriate people to consult about the characteristics of effective teachers were students. Letters were sent to 7,000 graduates (replies being received from just over 1,000), inviting them to name lecturers they could describe as excellent teachers, and to say what there was about these people and their teaching which made them effective. Once these outstanding lecturers were identified they were asked by Sheffield to contribute a chapter to his book, outlining how they went about teaching under-graduates. In addition, a further chapter, based on the responses of the 1,000 graduates, outlined the attributes judged to be characteristic of good teachers. Ten key characteristics of the effective teacher emerged from this data. To be worthy of such an accolade, he should be:

● master of his subject, competent
● prepare his lectures well, presenting them in an orderly way
● practical, able to relate his subject to life
● encourage students' opinion and questions

- enthusiastic about his subject
- approachable, friendly, available
- concerned for student progress
- possess a sense of humour
- warm, kind and sympathetic
- use teaching aids effectively

A relatively short list, but again rather daunting to the young teacher. Perhaps the major fallacy with this competencies or desirable attributes approach is the assumption that the way some particular experts themselves teach can or should be taught directly to those who are less experienced. It is apparent that Sheffield's list is more of a personality sketch than an objective description of teaching skills. This emphasis has emerged time and time again from studies which have attempted to analyse teaching effectiveness. Whereas investigators continually admit failure in identifying specific skills, competencies or practices which differentiate the good and bad teacher (eg Wilhelms, 1967), they are more successful in finding empirical support for personality differences. David Ryans (1964), for example, in a most exhaustive study of teacher behaviour was able to abstract three major dimensions:

Pattern Xo: Friendly, understanding, sympathetic, versus aloof, egocentric, restricted teacher behaviour.

Pattern Yo: Responsible, systematic, businesslike, versus unplanned, slipshod teacher behaviour.

Pattern Zo: Stimulating, imaginative, surgent, versus dull, routine teacher behaviour.

It is difficult to interpret such dimensions in terms of clear, easily definable competencies which could be taught to beginning teachers in an attempt to transform them into experts. Rather they seem to be integral aspects of personality, characteristic of the way a person operates over a wide range of human experience, not just in a teaching situation. It would appear that it is a matter of who a person is rather than what he does which is important to the development of his students.

Gilbert Highett (1951) in his beautifully written *The Art of Teaching* reflects this view when he draws attention to the importance of a teacher's human qualities. Though he must know and like his subject, the good teacher must make it relevant. This he does through making himself relevant. He feels that students normally learn a subject because they feel that the teacher's vitality and energy prove its value, rather than because they feel the compulsion of the subject matter itself. "The good teacher," according to Highett, "is an interesting man or woman."

Bugelski (1970) puts it another way, using the terminology of the psychologist. He invokes the theory of the conditioning of emotional responses, and applies it to teaching. Emotional responses (feeling good or bad) become attached to subject matter as a result of being paired with a liked or unliked instructor. Later the student will repeat and seek out subject matter which makes him feel good and avoid that which makes him feel bad or fearful. With a liked instructor, a student learns to approach a subject; with a disliked instructor a student learns to avoid it. Mager (1968) has cogently pointed out that learning is for the future, the object of instruction being to facilitate some form of behaviour after the instruction has been completed. The likelihood of a student applying his knowledge is influenced by his attitude for or against the subject — things disliked have a way of being forgotten. The teacher's influence, then, can be very important, and it seems desirable to have the student leave a course with as favourable an attitude as possible towards the subject. Possessing such an attitude, the student is likely to remember what he has been taught, and will willingly wish to learn more. Whether or not this favourable attitude is engendered seems to be a function of the sort of person the teacher is. This leads to a consideration of another way of looking at the good teacher.

## The Good Teacher Uses Himself Effectively

From the research into teaching effectiveness previously referred to, it would seem that this is a highly personal matter. The successful instructor attains this stature more by being the sort of person he is rather than by practising a set of competencies abstracted from the performance of other expert teachers. If good teaching can be seen as a function of a lecturer's personality, the definition of the effective teacher as a ". . . unique human being who has learned to use his self effectively and efficiently for carrying out his own and society's purposes" (Combs, et.al.: 1974. p.8) is worthy of careful consideration. Primarily, a good teacher is a person, a unique personality, who uses himself, his talents and his environment in such a way that he promotes learning amongst his students. This definition rejects the concept of the teacher as a technician applying, rather mechanically, the particular methods he has been taught or has picked up from his own experience as a student in favour of one which sees him as an intelligent human being, making use of his unique attributes to promote learning in those he teaches. In simple terms, the good teacher is the good person (Stanton, 1973) for his efforts are devoted towards helping others to develop their human potentialities.

Although this may seem a rather vague and nebulous concept, it is one which is in keeping with the reality of our experience. There exists no one particular style of good teacher, for there are so many ways we can use ourselves effectively. As we grow older, we learn more about ourselves, the things we can do well, the ways we can reach other people, and the good teacher seems to be a person who can use what he has flexibly, being willing to share himself with his students. Each of us is different, and so the ways in which we use ourselves will vary, yet certain attitudinal qualities, possessed to some extent by us all, seem to be of particular importance in promoting learning.

Carl Rogers (1969), drawing on his experience as an educator and a therapist, has attempted to define these qualities, claiming that the facilitation of learning virtually depends upon their existence in the teacher. The first of these is *realness* , the willingness to be a person and to live the feelings and thoughts of the moment. This involves dropping the role of "teacher" and revealing ourselves as we are, subject to the normal frailties and strengths of humanity. Secondly, the good teacher displays *acceptance*, being able to trust and respect the student for what he is. It is easy to condemn a student because he is not what we would like him to be, yet he needs to be seen as a separate person, valuable and worthwhile in his own right. Emerson put it succinctly when he said: "The secret of education lies in respecting the pupil." Rogers' third attitudinal quality is that of *empathy*, the ability to understand the students' reactions from the inside. This involves listening attentively to what our students say, giving them the opportunity to speak to us both verbally and non-verbally. We're not very good at this. Talking yes, listening no. Yet, as Epictetus pointed out many years ago, we have been given only one tongue but two ears, so that we may hear from others twice as much as we speak. To encourage learning, we should try to see things, as far as possible, from the viewpoint of our students, and this will involve curbing our natural verbosity in favor of more silent attentiveness.

I realize this intensely personal emphasis may seem just as fruitless as the "good scholar" or the "possession of competencies" approaches. To describe the good teacher as the "good person" and then attempt to affix some meaning to this concept could easily appear too idealistic to be of use. Providing a list of desirable personality characteristics is likely to be just as daunting as the competencies catalogues mentioned earlier. Yet the idea of a person using his unique attributes to facilitate learning does seem to me to provide a better basis for discussing the good teacher than the earlier concepts. My belief has been strengthened by research findings which highlight the personal aspects of the teacher. Such empirical evidence as is outlined below is far from conclusive, but it does seem more convincing than the assorted assumptions upon which the alternative approaches are based.

Hildebrand, Wilson & Dienst (1971) conducted a three year study at the University of California which involved a combined total of more than 1600 students and faculty. They found that excellent agreement existed between students, and between students and faculty, concerning the effectiveness of given teachers. Best and worst teachers engaged in the same professional activities and allocated their time among academic pursuits in the same ways, leading the authors to conclude that effective instruction was not assured by the mere performance of such activities. However, they were able to isolate five factors which differentiated the good from the bad teacher. One of these could be subsumed under the competency rubric, for it involved the organization of subject matter. The effective lecturer made himself clear, stated objectives, summarized main points, presented material in an orderly fashion and provided appropriate emphasis. This could also be considered an aspect of a person's character. Some of us are more systematic and well organized than others and teaching in this way is simply an expression of this innate characteristic. A second factor would support the "good scholar" approach for the effective teacher was seen as being in command of his subject, presenting material in an analytic way, contrasting varying viewpoints, and relating topics to other areas of knowledge. This too can be encompassed by the "self as instrument" concept. Our knowledge, just as our organizational ability is part of ourselves and as such is to be used to promote learning. All of the three remaining factors fall squarely within the orbit of the personality and could not be embraced by either the "good scholar" or "competencies" approach with any great degree of comfort. These describe the good teacher as:

(i)    encouraging lecturer-student classroom interaction. He is sensitive to the response of the class, encourages student participation, and welcomes questions and discussion.

(ii)   being willing to relate to students as a human being as well as a teacher. He is available to and friendly towards students, is interested in students as individuals, is himself respected as a person, and is valued for advice not directly related to the course.

(iii)  enjoying his teaching and making this enjoyment obvious to his students. He is enthusiastic about his subject, and makes the course interesting. Possession of self-confidence was also included in this context.

The authors of this study would not wish to claim that to qualify as a good teacher, a lecturer must possess all these qualities in abundance. They simply pointed out that their data indicated a general consensus by both faculty and students that these were seen as desirable attributes. The good teacher would be one who possessed such qualities and used himself in such a way as to encourage his students to learn.

The similarity between these findings and those of Sheffield (1974) quoted earlier is strong. In particular, it is clear that the best teachers are student oriented. They think students are important, they like them, and they respect them. Enthusiasm is perhaps the most obvious characteristic of their personality. Their love of teaching and of their subject is openly shared, both inside and outside the lecture room. This out-of-class interaction is very important. In his investigation into the effects of faculty on students, Gaff (1973) has stressed that the biggest difference between effective faculty and their non-effective colleagues is the extent to which they interacted with students outside the classroom. This is an interesting finding for earlier research (eg. Jacob, 1957) would suggest that lecturers are not normally influential in the lives of their students.

It would appear, then, we can answer the question: "Who is the good teacher?" The fact that the answer is given in terms of personality attributes rather than scholarship and competencies or technical skills is likely to be disturbing to many of us. Are teachers really born and not made? Is training a waste of time? There are no simple answers to these questions, still it does seem possible to help people use the qualities they possess more effectively and to assist them to grow as people. The "sensitivity group movement" is based on this assumption and my own experience would suggest that it has some validity in a teaching context (Stanton, 1976). This point will be considered more carefully a little later.

Acceptance of the view outlined in this chapter does entail a changed conception of how university and college teachers should be trained. Conventional emphasis on subject matter, knowledge and presentation skills require supplementation by personal growth experiences. As people learn more about themselves and their potentialities, they are normally more able to use themselves productively to help others. This, to me, is what teaching is all about.

# Chapter 4

# The "Best" Teaching Method

## Identification of the "Best" Method

The practical teaching problem in higher education is creation of an environment in which students may learn. One solution would be to identify that method of teaching which is "best" and use it on all occasions. Literally thousands of studies have been carried out in a fruitless search for this holy grail but, to date, it has stubbornly refused to reveal itself. Innumerable comparisons of one teaching method with another, under widely varying conditions, have been unable to guide educationalists in the formulation of an approach "best" for all teachers, all situations, all subjects and all students. Yet, the question continues to be asked. Might it be that the absence of an answer indicates that none is possible? The expectation of a single "best" method would seem to contradict the reality of human experience and its essential variability. Surely it is inappropriate if the view of teaching expressed in earlier chapters of this book is accepted. Good teaching and its concomitant, effective learning, seems so much a function of the teacher's personality that to seek a single approach applicable to all conditions is likely to be a useless activity.

Methods are means to an end. As Combs et.al. (1974) express it:
". . . the search for methods of teaching that are "good" or "right" for all teachers is fruitless. Modern psychology tells us that methods are but ways of accomplishing purposes. They are vehicles for achieving results. Whether their effects on others are good or bad depends on who is running the vehicle, what he is trying to do, and how this is perceived by those he is doing it to." (p.115).

The question, then, is not: "What is the best teaching method?" but: "What is the method most appropriate for this particular teacher teaching this subject to this class?" Such a reformulation is more complicated of course, and likely to be frustrating to the lecturer who wants an unequivocal answer. But there are few unequivocal answers in the realm of academia. That same lecturer, who would be appalled at attempts to reduce the complexity of research in his own subject discipline to a single general formulation, often demands this of the teaching methodology research. When it is not forthcoming he tends to damn the educationalists and condemn them for not knowing their field. He finds it unsatisfactory to be told that before he can decide on an appropriate method of teaching he needs to clarify his aims. That is, what is he attempting to achieve with his students? Unless we know where we are going, it is rather pointless attempting to get there as quickly as possible. Yet so many of us, when faced with this request to specify our objectives, are unable to provide answers. This greatly complicates selection of a teaching method. So too does the requirement that we need to be comfortable with the methods we use. No matter how successful a particular approach has been for others, unless it works for us and our students, it is inappropriate.

Broudy (1974) has argued that there are at least three distinguishable teaching styles, each embodied in rather different methods. The first of these is the didactic,

22

which aims at conveying those skills, knowledge and attitudes capable of being formulated explicitly with respect to outcomes and means. Lecturing may be particularly appropriate to achieve this. The second style is the heuristic with its emphasis on learning by discovery and problem-solving. Process rather than product is important here so discussion, laboratory work and independent study may all be appropriate teaching methods. Philetics is the third style. This incorporates modes of teaching such as experiential groups, peer discussion, and role playing which improve the relationship between lecturer and students, between student and student, and between the student and himself. Each of these three modes has distinctive outcomes, procedures and styles. Although combinations between them are often observed, at any one point in time only one occupies the focus. The others recede into the background. The issue here is the expectation that a lecturer should be equally competent and comfortable with all three teaching modes because they are highly correlated. This is just not so. Most teachers are fortunate if they are really good at one style. When forced to operate within the framework of the others they are far less effective. It is the "self as instrument" concept again. We are at our best when we use ourselves in the way or ways in which we are most effective. However, this is not to assert that we should find one approach that works and stick to it always under all conditions. We need to experiment, to try out different techniques, to find those which are most comfortable for us and those which promote learning among our students. But having done so, it seems self-defeating to persist with methods which are not working, even if other people extol their superiority.

This appears a reasonable position to take when we consider the multiplicity of variables involved in the teaching-learning process. There is no one best way of teaching any more than there is one best way of learning. Instead, there seems to be many best ways. The particular teaching approach used is, according to McKeachie (1964), dependent upon:

1. course objectives. Lectures may be effective for transmitting knowledge but not for encouraging critical thinking.

2. the instructor. Some instructors are enthusiastic . . . some are not.

3. the subject matter. Some materials may be especially suitable for lectures. Others may not.

4. the student. A type of student who profits from one method may do poorly when taught by an alternative method which is effective for another type of student.

This concept of an interaction between teaching method and student personality is an important one, particularly at a time when we are trying to pay more than lip service to the view that students are all different and should be taught as individuals. However, although the idea that different students are likely to perform better under different teaching methods is intuitively attractive and in accord with personal observation, research efforts have failed to offer any reasonable substantive support. Goldberg's (1972) massive study of trait-by-treatment interactive effect was fruitless at the tertiary level, and earlier attempts have had little more success. Wispe (1951), however, whose study really initiated serious research in this area, found that more than half of his sample (n = 160 college students) could be classified as "personality-insecure." These people required very structured situations so that tensions arising out of fear of doing the wrong thing could be reduced. They were most unhappy in permissive type teaching situations and performed best when their teachers were very directive.

Encouraged by this finding, and hints from other investigators that student personality characteristics influenced their learning under different teaching methods, I undertook a three-year study which involved using two instructional modes (Stanton, 1974a). One was highly directive lecturing which reduced students' work outside the classroom to a minimum. The other was a guided reading approach in which students received two preliminary course structuring lectures, a list of course objectives, appropriate references and sample examination questions. They had no further contact with me, being required to attain the objectives through their own reading and informal discussion with peers. Various personality scales were administered in an effort to identify which students did best under which method. Hopefully, I would then be able to use this data and present a course offered in at least two different ways, guiding students on the basis of their personality profile towards the method likely to be best for them. The efficacy of such an approach is dependent on clear cut differences emerging between the successful lecture method student and the successful guided reading student. This did not occur with sufficient strength to permit the diagnostic approach I sought, mainly due to the inadequacy of the standardized personality scales used (e.g. Cattell 16PF, EPI). However, use of a face valid scale (Stanton, 1972b) in which students were simply asked to report on their own perception of their personality characteristics proved more successful. The student likely to do well under a guided reading method emerged as relatively tense and anxious as compared with fellow students. This finding conflicts somewhat with that of Wispe who would suggest that the anxious student performs best under highly structured lecture conditions where he knows exactly what is expected of him. Although plausible explanations may be advanced for this disagreement, it does point up the relative lack of success achieved by attempts to match students to teaching methods. Despite theoretical arguments (e.g. Cronbach, 1967) about the necessity of such a matching, the practical basis for doing so does not, at present, seem to exist.

## Some Difficulties with Educational Research

Research has failed to help the cause of tertiary teaching in this area. Neither does it seem to have been outstandingly successful in providing guidance on the particular methods which work best under differing conditions. When one considers the decades of effort, the amount of resources, both human and financial which have been poured into this pursuit, the results are indeed meagre. Fincher (1970) has outlined the research problem clearly enough, but we seem to have done little towards finding an answer:

"No-one can rightly claim that programmed instruction is the "best" way for a student to learn. Indeed, if 60 years of research into the psychological principles of learning have established any final conclusion, it should be that there is no single best way to instruct or teach. To the contrary, we must conclude that students can learn under almost any condition imposed upon them. The point, therefore, is not whether students can learn under this condition or that type of instruction but, rather, under what conditions and under what methods of instruction can which students learn which subject matters or skills more effectively? This, in a nutshell, is the question for all concerned with education to tackle." (p.418).

The value of research in providing an answer to practical teaching problems has long been an article of faith in educational circles. One might well ask, in view of its minimal contribution to tertiary teaching methodology, how soundly based is such faith. Bloom (1966) has provided something of an answer. After a critical analysis of

24

70,000 studies listed in the *Review of Educational Research Journal* over a 25 year period, he concluded that only 70 were crucial or significant. Of the rejected studies, many failed to satisfy even minimal criteria for acceptability as adequate research while others, though methodologically sound, produced findings of no educational significance.

Mackie & Christensen (1967), in their review of psychological research, offer additional support for such a position. They feel that explicit quantitative analysis, even when technically adequate, does not take kindly to transplantation from laboratory to schoolroom, because the task conditions employed by the researcher bear no determinable relationship to tasks outside the laboratory. It is the old problem of setting up controlled conditions in an artificial environment which is then so unlike the real world situation that the findings are not generalizable. Microscopic studies, which is how most educational and psychological research might be described, have made very little contribution to the improvement of educational practices. (Oettinger, 1969).

The fault may not always be that of the researchers, for there are a number of reasons why it is difficult to find a definitive research-based answer to a question on teaching. For one thing, a search of all relevant data on a given question is very time consuming. Modern data retrieval methods will go a long way towards solving this particular problem but will not help in sorting out the confusion which arises from conflicting data. The discrepancies in the interpretation of such data by different educators and psychologists is a further source of confusion. We do tend to see things not as they are but as we are. Also, the interpretation of the same research studies can change with time, and in the light of more recent findings. Because of these conflicts, and the complexity of the whole teaching process, there are no unequivocal answers available (Biehler, 1971).

Why then do we bother with research? Perry London (1976), in a most amusing article, gives an answer which may not be as factitious as it seems:

"Looking back, it seems odd to say that we were trying to find out what was already known — that children are more susceptible to hypnosis than adults — but it is true. There were two main reasons for doing so: (a) it was a living, and (b) previous knowledge to this effect was not statistically elegant and not obtained by rigorous, precise methods that would permit everything to be compared at painful length to everything else. Any fool could have told you that children were better hypnotic subjects than adults, but no-one was in a position to bore you to death with the details. This was one of our main accomplishments." (p.113)

Fortunately, London never bores anyone to death and his work has been of great value in the field of hypnosis. So, although he and the other writers I have mentioned, may question the value of research, this does not mean that it has *nothing* to offer. Though its contribution may not be great in terms of the time, manpower and money expended, educational research can tell us *something* about teaching methodology.

## Research into Teaching Methods — Some Difficulties

The opinion expressed earlier in this chapter, that there is no "best" method, is not the only view possible. In fact, it would probably be a minority view if the realities of higher education are considered. Although many lecturers would subscribe to it in theory, their actual practice would refute it. I believe a person's behaviour is a better indication of his beliefs than are his words and the behaviour of university and college lecturers reflects the belief that there does exist a "best" method of teaching. This is the lecture. If the number of hours spent by students listening to lectures was compared to that spent in small group discussion, laboratory work and independent study, the former would far outweigh the latter in most institutions of higher education. This remains so despite research findings that lecturing is, under many circumstances, a poor teaching method. Again, this might be construed as a reflection on educational research, for even when it does produce reasonably definitive findings, relatively few people pay much attention. It may also be a reflection on the peculiar belief of academics that everything should be open to scrutiny and investigation except their own activities. Their behaviour says: "I know the best way to teach. I lecture. What research says about teaching in tertiary institutions is irrelevant, and I intend to continue doing things the way I always have." This is a gross generalization, but it does reflect a basic truth. Tertiary teachers' behaviour is governed by certain assumptions about teaching which bear little relation to empirical data.

When the mass of evidence relating to comparative teaching methods is considered, two main themes emerge (Dubin & Taveggia, 1968). The first of these, which is the more dominant, is the optimistic assumption that a scientific methodology could be applied to the analysis of comparative teaching methods. It has been assumed that by carefully applying experimental controls, the differences between two or more teaching methods could be objectively identified and the results measured, usually through examinations. The second theme relates to the search for an explanation of the "no significant differences" findings produced by most comparative method studies. To explain why different methods seem to produce similar examination performance, investigators often blame gross measuring instruments for their inability to detect "true" differences which "really" exist. It would be far more parsimonious to argue that there is not sufficient real difference between one teaching method and another to produce the desired and expected differences in measured outcomes. Yet, investigators find it hard to give up the belief that the varying inputs used have to produce significantly different outputs.

Stephens (1967) would resolve the issue quite easily. His theory suggests that 96% of the forces responsible for growth and learning are spontaneous. Therefore, the factors which are varied in an experiment can affect only the small fraction which remains and are hardly likely to produce discernible differences. Spontaneous tendencies account for most education, which happens naturally without rational deliberation. All that is needed is to bring an adult interested in academic material, and with a desire to communicate his interest, into contact with younger people. This being so, instead of worrying whether a pedigogical technique has unequivocal research evidence to support it, or whether it appears to be slightly more efficient than another, Stephens would suggest the teacher recognize that a variety of approaches have been shown to be equally effective. Hence he should feel free to choose those which fit his own personality or style — or the personalities and styles of particular students or groups of students.

Stephens is not alone in suggesting that experiments into different teaching methods have left intact the essential features of higher education. Gruber (1968) has pointed out that almost all the studies leave the following variables untouched: the student's academic work is divided into five or six courses per term; the teacher plans the course without consulting the student; the student is given no new orientation in the educational aim of becoming educationally independent; the student is given no specific instruction in active modes of thought which might transform his behaviour while studying; the immediate aim on which all students are necessarily focused is successful performance on a final examination and a satisfactory grade or mark in the course; and the person evaluating the student's performance is the teacher. When he operates within situations which are alike in all these essentials, the student studies in approximately the same way, whether the material is presented in the form of a lecture, conventional text-book, list of readings, or programmed text book. He decides what the lecturer wants him to know and he tries to learn it with a minimum of distraction.

Nachman and Opochinsky (1958) demonstrated this most effectively when they compared large and small classes. It was hypothesized that students in smaller classes, with more opportunities for discussion of difficulties, would do better in unannounced quizzes of classroom material than would students taught in large lecture groups. This hypothesis was confirmed. However, in a final examination for which the students could prepare, that is, they knew when it was to be and what material would be covered, no differences between the groups were found. The implication is clear. In studies comparing different teaching methods, testing should be unannounced. Waiting for a final examination, or any other announced test, gives students time to do extra study which effectively washes out any differences between the methods under examination.

## Educational Research — Some Findings

Given the difficulties and weaknesses so far outlined, it is still possible to abstract some reasonably well-supported findings from the research literature. One of these has been already discussed in terms of the "self-as-instrument" concept. It is not the actual teaching method which is so important. The important thing is *how* it is used, and this is a function of the sort of person the lecturer is. However, it is also very important to relate the method to the purposes for which it is to be used, and it is here that the findings of research can provide a very useful guide.

Costin (1972), in his review of the teaching method literature, *compared the lecture with discussion* in these terms:

1. Lectures do not consistently differ from discussion in terms of students' acquisition of information as measured by end-of-course examinations. Lecturing, then, would seem to be more efficient for facilitating this kind of learning on a time-cost basis.

2. Discussion is probably more effective than lectures for teaching cognitive skills, such as interpreting knowledge and solving problems.

3. Discussion may also be more effective than lectures for helping students retain information beyond the termination of a course, and for learning relatively difficult information.

4. As the emphasis on teaching a course moves from lecturing to discussion, students express more approval of the course.

Should this last point influence us in our choice of using either lecture or discussion? If we are thinking in terms of improved examination results, there is no need to do so for student preference is not related to the amount of knowledge they acquire (Asch, 1951; Faw, 1949; Stanton, 1974a). Yet, as Mager (1968) has pointed out, learning is for the future, and the likelihood of a student putting his knowledge to use once he has left university is influenced by his attitude for or against the particular subject: ". . . things disliked have a way of being forgotten" (p.11). It would seem, then, that there is some merit in teaching students in ways they prefer for, by so doing, the lecturer makes it easier for them to like his subject. As the actual learning outcome, measured by examinations, is similar for both lecturing and discussion, this would suggest an increased use of discussion methods. Costin, too, suggests more use of this approach on the grounds of combating students' complaints about the "impersonality" of their education.

However, this issue of which is best, lecture or discussion, is not the real point. It is not a matter of either-or, but of the appropriate balance to strike between the two approaches. This will vary in accordance with the particular course objectives. Where acquisition of knowledge is dominant, lecturing may assume a larger role than in a course which emphasizes problem-solving skills. It will vary, too, in terms of the teacher's ability to lecture and to lead discussion groups. No matter how desirable it may be to discuss, if a teacher is hopelessly inept in this situation and more effective lecturing, he should organize his teaching accordingly.

When *student-centred projects* are *compared with lecturing*, (Costin, 1972), no consistent differences between the methods are apparent. The effects of lectures, reading and self-instruction programmes on students' acquisition of information is comparable. This is true whether tests follow immediately after the learning experience or are delayed for some time. One factor which does emerge, however, is that of guidance. Unguided reading is normally inferior to lectures in helping students acquire knowledge, but when reading is guided through the use of questions and detailed references, it often becomes the more effective method. What does seem to be apparent is that the amount of time spent in the classroom is not significantly related to the achievement of students as measured by performance in final examinations and tests. Milton (1973) would take this point further by challenging the *assumption that a teacher is necessary in the classroom* at all. In support of this view he quotes the results of experiments indicating that students who attended no classes in an introductory psychology course, relying only on course outlines and textbooks, performed slightly better than students who: " . . . received the most exquisitely designed and executed instruction ever beamed at any group: all the exhortations which have been made through the ages about how to teach were followed assiduously three times per week." (p3). Evidence derived from comparisons of correspondence students with students taught more conventionally in a lecture situation, (Childs, 1952; Dysinger, 1957) provides confirmation of Milton's experience. My own experience (Stanton, 1972c) comparing a structured lecture course with one based on guided reading, would suggest that actual contact with myself contributed nothing measurable in a final examination. This may be, of course, a function of personal inadequacy, but naturally I prefer to think otherwise. Fortunately, the research literature provides abundant evidence that my experience was not unique. Once a course supervisor has planned a course, specified the objectives and listed the relevant references, he might well turn loose his students with no fears they would suffer — in terms of examination marks — through the lack of his presence in lecture or tutorial. It is arguable, of course, that a lecturer *may* provide stimulation, *may* help students to greater understanding, and *may* make material more interesting through his presence, but the evidence does suggest rather strongly that such gains are not reflected in conventional examination scores. The role of the lecturer as a face-to-face teacher has been over-exalted. If students can learn material just as effectively working by themselves, it would seem that many hours of lecturer and student time are being wasted as they sit "communicating" in the lecture room.

A lot depends, however, on the form this communicating takes. Much of the research literature defines it in terms of information transmitted. It is this communication which can be so easily replaced. Where the lecturer chooses to use himself as a resource available to students when they feel the need, the situation is different. This role of resource person has been related to the sequencing of instructional material by Mager (1961, 1969). He stresses the point that what appears as a "logical" organization of the subject matter for the instructor often appears quite illogical to the student. Results of a study conducted with adults learning electronics provided clear evidence of this. Permitted to generate their own syllabus, the students began at a point far different from that set down by the instructor, and the learning sequence they followed bore little resemblance to the normal syllabus. Yet results were better than in instructor controlled courses. Part of this success Mager attributed to a student being able to dictate the sequence of instruction most congenial to his own learning, and part to the role of the instructor as a "gap-filler". In a conventional lecture, the student draws on his own experience to fill the gaps in an instructional sequence and he does this without the knowledge of the lecturer. Under Mager's learner-generated sequence scheme, the student is able to indicate what gaps exist for him at a particular time and to seek help from the lecturer *at that time*. He is able to use the lecturer as a resource, a source of correct information at a time when he needs it.

## Wide Range of Methods Available

One thing which does emerge clearly from the research literature is the existence of a wide range of instructional methods. Although the bulk of the evidence would indicate that these all produce comparable results, this is not necessarily a good argument for ignoring alternatives to the accepted lecturing pattern. Despite evidence that groups of students, when their average examination marks are compared, do perform similarly under different methods of teaching, this is not true of individuals. Some students, for example, do learn more effectively when taught by guided reading than they do by lecturing. In the study mentioned earlier (Stanton, 1974a), I found that approximately 50 per cent of the students taking part performed differently when the teaching mode was changed. Some significantly improved their marks; some did significantly worse. Because the numbers revealing this change were approximately equal in either direction, improvement or decline, group averages remained the same, thus masking individual variability. To half the students in the experiment, teaching methods *did* make a difference. Observation of the students we teach confirms such a finding, for they do differ, responding well or poorly to the various approaches we use according to the sort of people they are.

Acceptance of this basic fact of human nature would lead to support of a procedure by which courses would be taught in a variety of ways. A lecturer could provide alternative modes, permitting students to succeed through employing the learning style they found most congenial. Unless choice is offered, students are all condemned to "learn" in the same way whether it is appropriate to them or not. Just as some teachers perform poorly in discussion groups but do well in the lecture room, so some students can probably learn by reading without attending lectures. All of them may not necessarily benefit from discussion. Some need self-paced opportunities. This all sounds very time consuming and exhausting for the lecturers who are asked to provide such learning alternatives. That it is more demanding than giving a lecture is certainly true. This provides one important reason for the widespread acceptance of lecturing as *the* way to teach. This popularity is, I believe, largely a result of laziness. Most of us like to adopt the easy way out and lecturing is the easy way out. We ignore the learning differences among students in the class and serve them up a predigested summary of our own reading, expecting them to learn it. Some do, some don't. If we provide alternative modes of teaching, we may be able to help some of the "don't's" to become "do's" and this would seem to be worth doing.

The fault, however, lies not only with the lecturer. Students are human too, and they like lectures as the easy way, for the work is often done for them. As long as they take down the important parts of the lectures, memorize these, and feed them back at examination time, a pass is assured. Not very stimulating or exciting — but easy. Yet, one of the most commonly affirmed aims of higher education is to help students think more independently, learning how to learn. Attempting to do so by reliance on lecturing as the basic teaching mode is unlikely to meet with much success. The lecturer's own teaching behaviour precludes such desirable outcomes.

This was brought home to me forcibly when I attempted to interest a group of graduate students in an independent study course. They were required to plan, carry out and evaluate projects without detailed guidance from other people. Although about two-thirds of the group, which numbered 90, were very much in favour of the idea, most of these expressed grave reservations as to their ability to satisfactorily complete such a course without regular, compulsory tutorials and assignment deadlines which would provide a basic timetable for them. They doubted their ability to take responsibility for their own learning, to program their own activities, to pace themselves. Yet these students were graduates who had successfully completed a three year university degree. If we are honest, most tertiary teachers will admit to many similar experiences. The much vaunted aim of fostering the independent learner is usually just that, an aim, one which is rarely translated into reality.

It is not enough, though, to criticise dependence on lecturing as the basic tertiary teaching mode. Alternatives must be provided. Several, such as group discussion, student-generated projects and reading have already been mentioned. A more comprehensive list emanating from the Learning Resources Program at the Utah State University is given below.

1. Exposition — Word
   a. Lecture
   b. Reading printed word
   c. Combination of both
   d. Tele-lecture

   Purpose: Data transmission.
   Motivate, explain
   Skill: Recall, reading
   Dangers: Students often limited to passive role

2. Exposition — Visual
   a. Film
   b. Filmstrip
   c. Slides

   Purpose: Transmit data
   Skill: Recall, visual perception
   Dangers: Students may be limited to passive role — no interaction

3. Question
   a. Recitation
   b. Problem solving
   c. Combination with lecture

   Purpose: Elicit student response
   Skill: Verbal, problem solving
   Dangers: Teacher domination; looking mainly for pre-set answers

4. Discussion
   a. Structured
   b. Inquiry exercise
   c. Student-initiated
   d. Bull session or casual conversation

   Purpose: Use or apply data, select from data, form opinions, social interaction
   Skill: Verbal expression, hypothesis forming, problem solving
   Dangers: Drifting from objective, domination by the uninformed, bluffing

| | | |
|---|---|---|
| 5. Group Processes<br>   a. Task groups<br>   b. Sensitivity sessions | Purpose:<br><br><br><br>Skill:<br><br>Dangers: | Human interaction, idea inputs<br>from many people, feedback from<br>many people, personality<br>development<br>Verbal expression, emotional<br>risk taking<br>Need a trained psychologist<br>as a leader to prevent psychic<br>damage to individual personalities |
| 6. Experiments<br>   a. Structured<br><br><br>   b. Unstructured | Purpose:<br>Skill:<br>Dangers:<br><br>Purpose:<br><br>Skill:<br><br>Dangers: | To illustrate processes<br>Recall, extrapolate<br>Students may memorize results<br>rather than understand process<br>To stimulate hypothesis<br>formulation<br>Initiating ideas, manipulating<br>apparatus<br>Very hard for student to<br>originate an experiment,<br>may just plagiarize |
| 7. Seminar | Purpose:<br><br><br><br>Skill:<br><br>Dangers: | To encourage students to<br>defend their own ideas based<br>on their own research in<br>confrontation with critics<br>Verbal expression, critical<br>analysis<br>Students may refuse to<br>criticise each other, teacher<br>may short-circuit the purpose<br>by dominating the discussion |
| 8. Simulation or Game<br>   Playing | Purpose:<br>Skill:<br><br>Dangers: | Student involvement<br>Use wits, takes risks, play<br>a role<br>Time consuming, may spend<br>all the time in game and none<br>in de-briefing |
| 9. Individualized instruction<br>   a. Programmed learning<br>   b. Audio-visual tutorial<br>   c. Listening programs<br>   d. Computer-assisted<br>      instruction | Purpose:<br><br><br><br>Dangers: | Transmit information, elicit<br>individual student response,<br>promote self-pacing, repetitions.<br>Reading or listening (or both)<br>Can become boring; some students<br>need teacher supervision; lacks<br>group interaction |
| 10. Direct Experiences<br>   a. Social drama<br>   b. Role playing<br>   c. Dramatization | Purpose:<br><br><br>Skill:<br>Dangers: | Get the students<br>personally involved in<br>creating the data<br>Empathy, spontaneity<br>Time limitations, can be<br>sabotaged by an unsympathetic<br>class |

| 13. Tests | Purpose: | To give students feedback on their learning |
| | Skill: | Writing and reading |
| | Dangers: | May measure test-taking skills more than knowledge |

| 11. Field Trip | Purpose: | To confront data in its real setting |
| | Skill: | Observation, classification, analysis |
| | Dangers: | Consumes much time in travelling |

| 12. Debate | Purpose: | For students to postulate and defend ideas in encounter |
| | Skill: | Verbal expression |
| | Dangers: | Winning becomes more important than learning |

| 14. Writing assignments | Purpose: | Students create, and express their own ideas |
| | Skill: | Written expressions, style interpretations |
| | Dangers: | Students may borrow or plagiarize |

| 15. Project | Purpose: | Practical ("hands on") experience often done outside class sessions |
| | Skill: | Organizing, carry through, verbal or written presentation |
| | Dangers: | Time consuming |

| 16. Case study | Purpose: | Discover concepts in narrative |
| | Skill: | Analytical thinking |
| | Dangers: | Students may fail to extract concept and only repeat the story |

| 17. Brainstorming | Purpose: | To generate many ideas, to involve the students in taking verbal initiatives |
| | Skill: | Verbal expression |
| | Dangers: | Verbal students may dominate |

| 18. Tutorial (one student — one faculty member.) | Purpose: | To engage a student in a confrontation where he presents and defends his idea with a faculty member |
| | Skill: | Hypothesis formulation, selecting data |
| | Dangers: | Time consuming for faculty |

Different learning methods do have differing strengths and weaknesses, so the attributes of each mode must be matched against course objectives, the type of material to be taught, the personality of the teacher, and the learning styles of the students. Achievement of a perfect match is highly unlikely but we can facilitate the learning of our students by at least making some attempt along these lines. To expect that one teaching technique can be stretched to cover all learning situations is, as Rockart (1973) puts it: ". . . to deny students the benefits of the application of the correct tool at the correct time. It is similar to a dentist who uses a single cutting bit, or a golfer playing with only his five iron". (p. 286).

# Chapter 5

# Effective lecturing

## Why Lectures are Criticized

It is now fashionable to trenchantly criticize lecturing. True, this method of promoting learning does give considerable scope for such attacks. In its normal form of a 50 minutes period of uninterrupted talk, there is no real opportunity for student participation, no student rehearsal of what is being taught, and no feedback to the lecturer on his effectiveness. As the lecturer proceeds, student performance declines sharply, such deterioration being noticeable as early as ten minutes after its commencement. Hall and Cannon (1975) quotes evidence suggesting that up to 70% of the material covered in the first ten minutes of a lecture can be recalled by students compared to only 20% of that "taught" in the last ten minutes. Further, the material which is recalled has a very short "memory life" if it is not applied immediately after the lecture. Students tested the day after a lecture remembered about half the material covered, but this was more than twice as much recalled by those who were tested several days later.

As well as pointing out that the formal lecture is a passive method of learning which gives students little opportunity to ask questions, critics stress its lock-step nature. All students receive the same content at the same pace. In addition, they are all exposed to only one teacher's interpretation of the subject matter with the attendant disadvantages of dullness and bias likely to become apparent. If the teacher's speech skills are poor, the lecture is likely to degenerate to the extent where it is unlikely to promote any learning at all. This is equally true if he is poorly organized and-or unaware of the reactions of students. In *The University Experience,* Little (1970) records the comment made by one of the students he interviewed:

" . . . then there's the type of person who sort of doesn't know where he is and just rambles on and on, and pays no attention to people." (p.39).

Another student stressed this inattention to what is actually happening in the lecture room when he said:

" . . . some appear to have no contact with the students, they just charge ahead when it must be patently obvious to them that no one understands a word of what they're saying." (p.39).

This obsession with covering the ground whether students are able to understand the material or not has already been mentioned and is really a deficiency of the lecturer rather than of the lecture itself. Yet, it is difficult to separate the person from his teaching method. Perhaps the 50 minute, uninterrupted speech format imposes constraints which are difficult to transcend.

Schonell et. al. (1962), for example, list the most important causes of dissatisfaction with lectures in this way:

(a) lecturer incoherent
(b) lecturer gave too little or too much detail; he failed to emphasize main points

34

(c) lecturer failed to come down to student's level

(d) lecturer spoke badly

(e) lecturer made it very difficult for the student to take notes

(f) lecturer was dull and uninspiring because he merely read his own notes

(g) lecturer's writing and diagrams on the board were too small — too crowded or unreadable.

It would seem that most of these faults could be rectified in a situation where the channels of communication between lecturer and students were reasonably open, where feedback could be given and received. Yet, it is in this respect that the formal lecture is suspect, for it is normally a one-way communication process. The weakness of such a process has been made apparent by Brown and Henderson (1972). They describe the situation in which two people were placed at opposite ends of a telephone line in different rooms. One person had a set of dominoes before him, arranged in an irregular but simple pattern. Before the other person was a similar set of dominoes, not arranged in any pattern. The object of the experiment was to have this latter set put in the same pattern as the first, on the basis of one way instructions given by the person sitting before the first set. No questions or requests for additional information were permitted, nor was it possible for instructions to be repeated. Despite numerous repetitions of this experiment, not once was the second pattern correct. The experiment was subsequently re-run with ample opportunity for questions and feedback. Under the conditions, the second pattern was always right.

The moral here would seem to be that it is the non feedback, non participatory nature of the formal lecture which accounts for its ineffectiveness as a learning medium. Although critics blame the lecturer for this state of affairs, students too must bear some responsibility. Postman and Weingartner (1971) have commented that students possibly prefer lectures because the expectations placed upon them are simplified. All that is asked of them is to sit passively and write down as many of the lecturer's words as possible. There is no obligation for them to take any of the risks inherent in debate and discussion. According to Postman and Weingartner, all students really learn in lectures is to respect authority, to confuse notemaking ability and memory skills with genuine intellectual growth, and to view intellectual life as essentially a passive enterprise. True, it may be argued that we have made students passive non-participators, yet students are able to force changes if they care enough to do so. But why should they? As has been previously pointed out, the lecture is easy for them. No real intellectual effort is required, the lecturer does all the work of material collection and synthesis. All they need to do is take notes and memorize them. Basically the responsibility is ours for distorting the stated aim of fostering independent learning through reliance on a teaching method which actively discourages such behaviour, but students must bear some responsibility for permitting such a situation to exist.

They have a responsibility, too, in a quite different way. One of the main claims made by supporters of the lecturing method is that it does have certain advantages as an information transmittal medium. Though the type of content transmitted, may be open to criticism, they see the actual method as economical and efficient. Yet even here, the one-way nature of the communication is suspect, for students seem to lack the basic skills required in the area of "listening". Perhaps it is part of a lecturer's task to teach students how to listen, how to perceive the structure of a lecture, how to take notes effectively; but students, too, need to cultivate these skills actively themselves. Unless they do so, they are unlikely to receive much of the information being transmitted. So the evils of the lecture format are compounded. Not only does it encourage passive dull students, but it may also be ineffective in passing on course content to students who lack appropriate "listening skills". This is, however, a highly debatable area, with claims that lectures are an inefficient means of conveying information (eg. Hall-Cannon, 1975) being contested by those who see this method as quite adequate to accomplish such a purpose (e.g. Costin, 1972).

Despite this particular conflict of views, the weaknesses of the lecturing method outlined so far in this chapter might lead one to conclude that the days of the 50 minute uninterrupted speech are numbered. With so much against it, how can the formal lecture continue as the main vehicle of university and college instruction? With our normal propensity to swing from one extreme to another, there are now calls for the complete abolition of lectures, demanding their replacement by discussion groups and independent study. This seems as unrealistic as claiming the lecture to be the best teaching method under all conditions. Some balance between the two viewpoints seems necessary, looking always at the objectives of instruction for, in many ways, lecturing remains a valuable teaching approach. The mere fact of its survival over such a long period would suggest that it may embody powerful virtues and it is to a consideration of these that we now turn.

*Strengths of the Lecture Method*

Again, it is difficult to separate the person from the method. Although, as has been previously pointed out, the lecture format does impose certain limitations on the teacher, it is a tool and, as such, capable of misuse. Criticism is often more of an attack on how the lecture is used or misused rather than upon the method itself. A good lecturer can promote learning among his students even when using it to achieve apparently inappropriate ends. A poor lecturer is unlikely to do so, no matter how suitable his method is matched to the ends he seeks. Unfortunately relatively few academics lecture well, for soundness of preparation and excellence of scholarship count for little if the lecturer is inaudible, incoherent or insensitive to his audience. Perhaps the method does have serious constraints but it is possible, working within these, to promote effective learning.

Fitzgerald (1968) is one who has pointed out how this might be done by indicating an area where the lecture can be used most fruitfully. He specifies three aspects of teaching a subject. The first of these is exposition, whereby the lecturer's intention is to give students a factual account of the basic subject matter. Methodology is the second, with instruction in the techniques or skills of a subject being its key aspect. Helping law students argue the way lawyers do would be an example. The third aspect, and to Fitzgerald, the most important, is what he calls criticism, though the term is interpreted very broadly. It involves the notion of students being encouraged to realise that the latest developments in their subject are tentative frontiers only, that they have the obligation to question what they are told and what they read, and to inquire, even more basically, whether their discipline is asking the right questions. This is the very essence of higher education and it is in this context, Fitzgerald claims, that the lecture reigns supreme, unchallenged by any alternative teaching approach. Only within the lecture situation can the teacher present a model of the thinker in action, the enthusiastic searcher after truth. This is because the lecture provides the opportunity for the lecturer to teach not only his subject but himself. Again, the personal qualities of the instructor emerge as vital. The teaching mode provides the opportunity to achieve the ends Fitzgerald sees as so important, but whether the opportunity is used to promote effective learning is a function of the individual.

Method is important, however. The lecture format *helps* the student learn to be "critical" whereas it is less facilitative in the expository aspect and quite unhelpful for instruction in the techniques of a subject where students must learn to do things for themselves. There is an interactive relationship here between lecturer, method and purpose which makes nonsense of sweeping generalisations about "best" teaching methods.

In their eagerness to dispose of lectures entirely, critics overlook other strengths, not only that given above relating to the model of the truthseeker. Engaging in a university or college course is not a solitary activity. Rather it is more of a corporate venture and the lecture provides the forum in which all course participants come together to share a common experience. Whether they participate actively or not, by their very presence they become part of something greater than themselves. If the lecture is basically inspirational in nature, they are given the opportunity to share the instructor's enthusiasm and love of his subject, and somehow, this seems easier to attain in a large group setting. Where the lecture is more didactic, this corporate enthusiasm may be less apparent but the sensitive instructor can still create among his students a feeling of belonging, of being part of a social group.

Probably more common than either the purely inspirational or the purely didactic is the lecture which combines elements of both. Used effectively, such a lecture is likely to embody some, at least, of the following advantages (Laing, 1968).

- Many students, owing to their immaturity, are likely to learn more easily from listening than by reading. Although this is a largely untested assumption it does fit with the evidence reported earlier (Stanton, 1974a) that different students learn best under different teaching methods. Some thrive on reading, others on structured lectures.

- Lectures can provide a valuable way of introducing and opening up a subject to a student. This is particularly true of one likely to daunt the student through the apparent difficulty of its content. Unassisted reading is unlikely to provide an answer in this situation, and may rob the student of the desire to enter a new field. This is an important consideration when related to earlier discussion on broadening of student interests. One stance frequently adopted by educational theorists is that students should be taught only those things which interest them (e.g. Rogers, 1969). Adoption of such a position denies them the opportunity of developing new interests. The "opening up" lecture can achieve this more effectively than other methods if it is infused with the lecturer's love of, and involvement in, his subject.

- Further, the lecture can provide the signposts which enable the student to find his way through rapidly expanding fields of knowledge or through very complex material. Without such direction he can too easily lose the wood for the trees, becoming hopelessly emeshed in unnecessary detail. This is particularly true in an area where so much material has been published that the student can become easily overwhelmed.

- The converse is also true. If there is relatively little published material in an area, the lecture may provide the necessary elaboration, providing a more up-to-date and balanced survey of the field.

In practical terms, lecturing is a teaching mode economical of staff time. Given all the possible merits of the method outlined above, this is probably the main reason why it is still so prevalent and why it is likely to continue to be so. A lot of information may be transmitted quickly to many students at the same time. In his study into the use and misuse of learning materials, Roe (1975) had this to say:

"It is often alleged that lecturing and attending lectures are inefficient methods of teaching and learning ; attention span is brief, the material is mostly available and can be more efficiently learned elsewhere, the lecturer himself has shortcomings as a communicator. It seems, however, on the evidence produced in this exploratory study, that a higher proportion of student contacts with teaching-learning materials may be useless. It may be that even more time and effort is wasted by students this way than when they are (however sporadically) listening to lectures or listening and talking at tutorials — and that even less learning takes place." (p.79).

As I have indicated this is one popular viewpoint, that more independent learning methods may be inferior to the lecture. So much seems to depend, however, on *how* the material is transmitted in lectures. All the advantages outlined earlier depend on this. We really have no excuses for bad lectures. A lecture *may* arouse, stimulate, give perspective on a subject, prepare the way for discussion, exhibit a way of thinking, and dramatically present a flow of ideas in a way no other method of teaching can do. Yet so often it fails to do so. Perhaps this is partly due to our lack of knowledge about ways in which lectures can be made more effective learning experiences for the students who attend them. Consideration of these may help us approach more closely the view of the ideal lecture which has emerged in the preceding pages.

## Secrets of Master Lecturers

In a study of academics reputed to be outstanding lecturers Davis (1965) identified two major techniques which he felt were the reasons for their success. Although each of three professors he observed was well-informed, enthusiastic, sincere, respectful of his audience, and clearly audible, Davis concluded that the two things which were strikingly similar and especially effective in their teaching were:

1. simplicity of the lecture plan, and
2. abundant use of examples.

When I read this conclusion, my first reaction was that it seemed too simple. Accustomed to voluminous lists and detailed analyses of the teaching process, I was loath to accept such a formulation. Yet, as I continued my own observations of the lecturers I was advising, and as I recalled my earlier experiences in the education of high school teachers, I realised that Davis had successfully abstracted two key elements marking the effective instructor.

His first point, simplicty of lecture plan, refers to structure. Most of the really successful lecturers I have observed restrict their lectures to three or four main points. These are made very clear to students as the essentials of the lecture, all else being subsidiary elaboration. With such an uncluttered format, the lecture is normally easy to understand. Notemaking if facilitated, too, for the key points are used as headings under which the detail may be easily subsumed. Such detail frequently takes the form of examples, Davis' second point. Often, the successful lecturer draws on his personal experience as a source of illustration, or uses experiences likely to be common to his audience. Each of three or four key points of the lecture is illustrated in this way, with several different examples being used to clarify the particular issue. Such illustrations might be verbal, or visual, or a combination of both. This technique promotes student learning by helping them relate the new information to their own experience and previously existing knowledge. It also creates a more informal, relaxed classroom atmosphere, for the lecturer is sharing something of himself, interacting with his students in a more personal way. By so doing, he is able to humanize his academic material, making his lectures more lively and interesting. If a lecturer insists on covering too much material, and tries to make his many points without the use of frequent and relevant examples, he runs a grave risk of being turgid, dull and pedantic. Therefore, it would seem that the first step towards improvement of the lecture as a teaching method is attention to the way it is structured.

## Structure of a Lecture

In his interesting little book entitled, *Lecturing,* Powell (1973) sets out several basic structures which are well worth considering. The first of these he refers to as the *classical structure.*

*Opening* A concise outline of the sequence of the lecture based on its objective. (Powell suggests this objective should be stated in behavioural terms, a point to be considered in more detail in a later chapter).

*Body* Statement of first idea. Development (the use of examples would be very useful at this point).
Restatement
Statement of second idea
Development. Restatement of first and second ideas
Statement of third idea
Development. Restatement of first, second and third ideas.

*Conclusion* Restatement of opening.

As Powell says, this structure is both simple and elegent. Although the number of ideas presented in the body of the lecture may vary, they should, as has been previously emphasised, be few in number, enabling the structure to be quite evident to students. This approach embodies the recipe attributed to a successful American coloured preacher: "First, I tell them what I'm going to tell them, then I tell them, and last I tell them what I've told them."

A second useful structure is the *scientific.*

*Opening* Statement of scientific objectives.
*Body* Data upon which interpretations might be based.
Various interpretations of this data.
*Conclusion* Lecturer's summing up of interpretations.

In this case the nature of the subject matter virtually determines the structure for the basic purpose of the lecture is to outline a particular sequence of activity leading to a scientific conclusion.

The *persuasive structure* is the third outlined by Powell.

*Opening* Statement of a speaker's point of view
*Body* Arguments against the speaker's point of view
Demolition of these arguments
Arguments favourable to the speaker's case
*Conclusion* Restatement of speaker's point of view.

There is some doubt whether, in a persuasive lecture, we should present our own views first or give primacy to the opposing argument. To a great extent, this probably depends on the audience. If they are likely to be relatively hostile and opposed to the lecturer's viewpoint, it is probably preferable to present the opposing case first. Where the audience is more friendly and in tune with our ideas, begin with these. Which ever order is used, it is important to explicitly state your conslusions, not leaving students to infer these from the arguments you present. This structure may not, of course, seem applicable in the context of a university or college. We do not normally seek to persuade but rather to present material more objectively, setting up the conditions under which students are helped to think independently. Still, there are occasions, particularly when we are discussing an area of research in which we are highly involved, that we do use persuasion. Under these conditions it is preferable to openly admit to yourself what you are doing and, if you still wish to do so, structure your lecture to maximize your chances of doing it well.

The way these three lecture structures have been set out seems to imply conventional lecture presentation of 50 minutes continuous exposition, but this is not necessarily the case. Such a procedure, as has been already pointed out, is a most inefficient method of facilitating learning. A more suitable approach is to break up the lecture into a number of shorter segments, thus allowing for variety and a change of activity. Lloyd (1968), in his study of student knowledge assimilation in conventional 50 minute lecture, has suggested that the most effective use of teaching time might be achieved by the concentration of effort in the following directions:

| | |
|---|---|
| initial period (0-5 minutes) — | quick establishment of compatibility |
| early period (5-10 minutes) — | high pressure transmittal of vital information |
| early middle period (10-20 minutes) — | recapitulation, consolidation, and illustration |
| middle period (20-40 minutes) — | further consolidation and development at relaxed pressure allowing recuperative periods. Descriptive and illustrative. |
| early final period (40-45 minutes) — | sharp increase in transmission pressure for short duration |
| late final period (45-50 minutes) — | relaxation of transmission pressure — probably best reserved for items demanding visual attention and not requiring notetaking, e.g. giving further illustrations, handing out reading lists, inviting questions. |

Although this way of organizing a lecture is a helpful guide to the effective use of the 50 minute period, it does not provide much assistance regarding the varying of activities within the specific segments. Such variation is a key point unemphasized by Davis in his analysis of the secrets of master lecturers though it was implied in much that he said. The lecturer desirous of increasing the learning of his students would be well advised to deliberately plan for different activities at different stages of his lecture. One such plan might look like this:

(1) Distribution of duplicated sheets, such *handouts* containing information which might include a list of objectives to be achieved, key points to be covered, and references.

(2) *Outline* of the lecture's structure stressing key points. This preview need not be spoken but might take the form of a summary written on the blackboard or an overhead projector transparency.

(3) *Lecture session* wherein one or two of the basic points listed in the overview are elaborated. Visuals may again be employed, for if key points are presented by

means of 35mm slides or overhead projector transparencies, the lecturer is freed from his notes and can speak more informally. He has the material available on the screen to refer to as he develops his theme.

(4) Few minutes of *student activity.* This may take the form of a discussion between pairs of students, a buzz group where 3 or 4 students particpate or even a period of silence in which notes are reviewed.

(5) *Lecture session* to develop the remaining key points, using examples both verbal and visual.

(6) *Student activity,* perhaps a problem solving task.

(7) *Summary* of the important points and check on the achievement of lecture objectives.

Such a structure overcomes the biggest problem of the 50 minute uninterrupted monologue, for student activity can be organised to provide two-way communication.

## The Development of Two-way Communication in Lectures

### 1. The Lecture Discussion

Transforming the formal lecture so that it permits student participation is not a difficult task. One way of doing so is a method referred to as lecture-discussion. This can take many forms, one of the most popular being to commence the session with a series of questions. As students provide answers, these are written on the blackboard. Further questioning and information provided by the lecturer contributes a continuing elaboration of this material. Too often we presume our students to be quite ignorant about the information we intend to present. By initially drawing forth their knowledge, we permit them to contribute to the lecture while avoiding the danger of boring them with material they already know. What occurs in this approach is a constant give and take between lecturer and students, the resultant information being organised on the blackboard or overhead projector as it develops. It is a shared activity which helps to shift the emphasis from the lecturer doing most of the work to admitting the students as partners in the quest for knowledge.

An alternative strategy is to use the first half of the lecture time to present new information and important principles. The second half of the period would be used for class discussion led by the lecturer or particular students who are selected for their knowledge of the topic under consideration. Discussion could be about the soundness of the principles presented, weaknesses of theory or supportive evidence, further research required to fill in gaps, problems likely to arise from an application of the principles or generalizations, and ways these might be overcome. The particular areas of discussion will vary according to the subject matter but the teaching principle does provide certain advantages lacking in the formal lecture.

Much of its success depends on the *questioning skill* of the lecturer. Open type questions for which there is no one correct answer are more likely to involve students than those requiring a single convergent, accepted answer. Closed questions such as: "When did the Second World War commence?" require students to only recall or recite. Open questions such as: "Why do wars occur?" permit a wide range of student responses, all of which are likely to be correct in one way or another. The threatening nature of the situation is reduced because there is far less chance of being wrong. Answering incorrectly, particularly if this response provokes a sarcastic rejoinder from the lecturer, can be very humiliating to a student and he is normally reluctant to take such a risk. Questions that ask for opinions, feelings and ideas evoke a far greater response than those which ask for precise factual information and therefore they are more helpful in promoting discussion.

41

It is necessary to be prepared for silence, particularly when the class you are teaching is not used to you. They have probably been well conditioned as passive listeners and the unaccustomed participation you are requesting of them is likely to come as somewhat of a shock. If you become nervous during the few seconds of silence following your question, you are strongly tempted to rephrase it, or answer it yourself. Realising this, your students will simply sit back and let you continue your monologue. Demonstrate by your behaviour that you are willing to wait, and to accept all answers. If an answer is wrong, ask further questions using it as a springboard to probe deeper. As your students become more comfortable in the situation, they will tend to contribute far more readily, often generating further questions of their own.

## 2. Buzz Groups

Another way of varying the lecture format through encouraging student discussion is the buzz group. Such groups normally comprise four or five students who are sitting together in the lecture room. The instructor asks students to form such groups by having alternate rows swing around in their seats so they may talk easily to those seated behind them. Normally a problem is posed and the groups are given time to discuss possible solutions. Or they might be asked to decide on certain criteria for the evaluation of concepts presented earlier in the lecture. As lecture theatres are not usually noted for their comfort, particularly when some students will be sitting in their seats the wrong way around, such buzz-group activity is kept rather short, perhaps only four or five minutes being used in this way. The lecturer may wander around the room while the discussion is in progress, getting some idea of the range of suggestions being advanced. At the end of the period allotted, the lecturer has representatives of various groups report back to the class as a whole. Not every buzz-group needs to contribute. Probably there will be a lot of overlap in their solutions and once the basic ones have been reported, other groups may simply provide additions. For successful use of this technique, it is important for students to be told very clearly what they are to discuss, how they are to report back and how the groups will be formed. Where the physical environment of the lecture room makes turning around difficult and uncomfortable, you may find it necessary to restrict the discussion to pairs of students sitting side by side. It is preferable, however, to use the slightly larger group where this is possible.

Usually the problem the buzz-groups are working upon is verbally presented by the lecturer. This does not have to be the case. An alternative is to prepare a series of 35 mm slides or overhead projector transparencies in the form of multiple choice questions. One of these could be used for each of the important points covered in the lecture. The lecturer speaks about the particular principle and then projects the multiple-choice question on the screen. The buzz-groups discuss the alternatives and attempt to agree on the correct answer. These answers are then announced to the whole class and the reasons for different choices discussed. Another way of using this technique is to project the slide first, before any discussion of the principle whatsoever. Buzz-groups then announce their answers and, in the ensuing discussion, misinterpretations and errors can be identified and corrected. This approach is based on the concept of making learning meaningful by first arousing a need to know in students then providing the means by which they can meet this need. It avoids the situation characteristic of much teaching where students are given information before any need has been aroused to seek that information.

This technique of presenting multiple-choice questions visually does not have to be tied to buzz-groups. The entire lecture may be programmed around the use of such visuals. Students are provided with a duplicated sheet on which all questions are given, and then, as each slide is projected, choose the answer they feel is correct and mark it on their sheets. After the lecturer takes a few answers, he then explains why certain answers are correct and others incorrect. Two-way communication is constant throughout the lecture when such an approach is adopted. Use of the handout question sheet seems to contribute considerably to the success of the technique. Handouts, too, have been mentioned earlier in the discussion of lecture structures so it should be of some value to consider their function in more detail.

## The use of handouts

When the structuring of lectures was under consideration duplicated handouts were seen primarily as a means of providing the preview of key points, of setting out objectives, and of indicating appropriate reference material. Such a preview would seem valuable in facilitating student learning, providing a clear statement of what was expected of them. It is particularly useful to couch the statement of objectives in a form similar to the following:

After attending this lecture you should be able to:
1. distinguish between internal and external frames of reference;
2. explain what is meant by the term "self-concept";
3. outline the importance of the "self-concept" as a determinant of human behaviour;
4. explain three ways in which the "self-concept" might be changed.

When objectives are expressed in such a way, students know what they should be able to do by the end of the lecture. If they are unable to do so, they realise they must seek additional information, either from the lecturer, fellow student or reference books. The lecturer who clarifies expectations in this way is likely to promote more successfully learning amongst his students than one who leaves his aims undefined.

Handouts can, however, serve a much wider purpose than the rather limited one outlined above. In an article on the notetaking ability of students, Hartley and Marshall (1974) have pointed out the generally poor level of skill exhibited. This was particularly true of first year students who were able to note only about eleven per cent of the material transmitted by the lecturer. They suggested that students should be given instruction in notetaking strategies, be told by lecturers when it was desirable to take notes, and be given handouts, either in skeleton form or as complete lecture scripts, perhaps with space being left to enable additions during the lecture.

The question raised by Hartley and Marshall, involving the comparative value of duplicated handouts and student made notes, is one worthy of serious consideration. Freyberg (1956) studied four different ways by which lecturer material could be received by students. These were: (1) taking no notes, (2) writing full notes, (3) making an outline, and (4) accepting a duplicated summary. Taking no notes proved most successful when material was to be used almost immediately, suggesting that notemaking may interfere with understanding of the lecture. However, when material was to be used at a later date in the answering of examinations, duplicated notes were the most effective. Whether such notes should be skeleton outlines or full lecture scripts was not considered in Freyberg's study, but this distinction has been made by others.

Klemm (1976) handed out incomplete, skeleton notes in a Biology course. His aim was to provide a framework helping students to organise their own notemaking more effectively and to give them more time to participate in, and think about, the lecture. It was necessary for the student to re-phrase the words the instructor used in the skeleton notes and to provide missing information. The notes were brief, emphasis falling upon key words designed to stimulate mental pictures for the students. Improved learning resulted from this use of handout material according to Klemm. He concluded that the "bare-bones" of a subject should not be transmitted verbally, but directly by means of handouts. Because these notes are ideally organised according to the lecturer's priorities, stripped of unessentials and easy to read, student study time can be lessened. A side effect might well be to assist them take notes more effectively in other courses.

Elton (1970) would go further, suggesting that first year science students value notes giving a detailed coverage of an entire course. Such handouts enable them to follow lectures better and to revise more effectively. Teaching staff benefit from such an approach, too, for they are able to modify their courses on seeing overlap with the material presented by a colleague. The problem with such complete handouts is students staying away from lectures. After all, they have the notes so why should they attend? Such a problem is largely illusory according to Elton who found little evidence that circulation of duplicated notes induced laziness or absenteeism.

This finding was confirmed by Nolan (1974) in a psychology course where he issued complete notes to his students. These students were told the examinations would be based entirely on the handout notes and the set readings, but that the lecturer would be present every session, available for discussion and questioning. Attendance at these sessions was optional. This procedure was compared with a conventional lecture course, no difference in examination results being observed. An interesting point made by Nolan concerned students staying for more discussion sessions when notes were handed out all together at the start of a course than when they were distributed on a lecture by lecture basis.

These ideas about the use of handouts material complement the earlier discussion on changing the communication pattern in the lecture. Such material provides a useful base for the two-way communication procedures where students participate actively in lectures. Freed from the necessity of making copious notes, they are more able to interact with the lecturer, so avoiding the main disadvantage of this teaching method. This principle of using full lecture scripts as handouts can — and has been — extended even further. Instead of suggesting them as a basis for a two-way classroom communication, MacManaway (1970) sees them as an alternative to lectures. Students could study them in their own time in place of lecture attendance, the time saved being used to increase the number of tutorials and seminars based on material provided in the lecture scripts. This viewpoint relates back to an earlier theme, that students learn information just as well from their reading as they do from listening to a lecture. Most lecturers would claim they do both, providing material in their lectures and referring students to additional information in books. The form these assigned reading handouts take, however, requires considerable care.

In a detailed analysis of the reserve book collection at the University of Alberta, Marshall (1974) found students making more extensive use of multiple short reading lists which assigned material in small amounts, than they did of the traditional long reading list handed out at the beginning of a course where the material was assigned all at once. Marshall's finding accords quite well with other information relating to students' reading habits. If only one or two key books or articles are set as additional reading, the work is likely to be done. However, if a long reading list is handed out, it is unlikely that students will read anything at all. The enormity of their task is too daunting.

Assuming the lecturer has set a reading list which is short, there are other things he may do to encourage students to actually read the material he suggests. That such encouragement is needed emerges clearly from a study by Hartley and Cameron (1967). In their experiment, they found that students regarded lectures primarily as providing a framework of ideas and theories into which subsequent work could be fitted. Students claimed they would follow up lectures with reading to fill in the factual information. This just did not happen — intention to read further was not translated into action. To improve on this undesirable situation, perhaps the lecturer might read short extracts as trailers to arouse interest or summarise main points.

Explicit reference to assigned reading in lectures is helpful, particularly when students have been asked to prepare themselves in this way. When students' behaviour reveals they have done their reading reward them with your attention and a word or two indicating your recognition of their work. Don't ignore this behaviour for that is the surest way to ensure its cessation. However, as well as referring in lectures to the reading set, ensure that students are able to actually get hold of the material. Complaints of library staff against the all-too-common practice of lectures dashing off reading lists without consulting them are legion. Frequently such lists not only lack sufficient information about what is expected of students but also make reference to books and articles which are either unavailable or not available in sufficient quantities. If we consider a reference important enough to place on a reading list, our behaviour should reflect this. Making sure it is available is essential, but it is also necessary to emphasise its value. In fact, the use of emphasis generally is of importance at many stages in a lecture.

## The use of Emphasis

Students' learning can be greatly facilitated if lecturers help them to remember key points. Having students respond in some way and reinforcing their response is valuable but it is essential that their attention be focused on the key point when it is first presented. This can be achieved through emphasising its importance in various ways. Possibly the most obvious of these is through voice variation. We can stress a fact by speaking more loudly, or more quietly. A few seconds' pause before the point is made is particularly effective in focusing attention. This effect can be enhanced by repeating the point a second time. Use of the voice as a punctuation device is also of value in marking transition stages in a lecture. When one argument or theme has been finished, pause before raising the next issue.

The blackboard plays its part in focusing attention. Difficult names, formulas and dates should always be written down, but so too should the salient points of the lecture. Students thus see the structure taking shape before their eyes and this is valuable even if they have it already before them in the form of a handout. Use of the blackboard in this way may be coupled most effectively with vocal cues. For example, consider the lecturer who speaks thus: "This procedure has four aspects. First, it should ensure the ATTENTION of the student." As the lecturer finishes his sentence he pauses, then writes "1. Attention" on the blackboard. This might sound very "schoolroomish" but unless students are cued as to what is important in a lecture they can easily become lost in a maze of apparently unrelated facts.

Eye contact is valuable here, particularly if associated with a pause in the lecturer's speech flow. As he stops speaking, he allows his eyes to move slowly over the whole group of students, then makes his point emphatically. Eye contact is not, of course, restricted only to the preparation of students for an important statement. It is essential to the building of rapport. Many lecturers speak to the lectern on which their notes rest, to the blackboard, or to the upper corners at the rear of the lecture room, never permitting their eyes to rest on the students to whom they are presumably directing their words. By doing so, they create a quite unnecessary barrier, for their behaviour sets them far apart from the students who feel no real sense of inclusion in the lecture. Unless a lecturer looks at his students he gains no idea of how his lecture is being received. Are they excited, bored, puzzled, wanting to ask a question? Such feedback can create a certain flexibility in subject matter, content and presentation style as the lecturer adapts to his audience's response.

Normally lecturer-class rapport will improve as students feel this sensitivity in their mood. Such rapport may be heightened through the use of a very simple technique. Select six or eight students seated in widely separated parts of the theatre and, at some time during the lecture, make a point of looking directly at each one of them. Because of the lecturer's distance from the class, his eyes will embrace not only the particular student picked out but also many of those seated around him. By using his gaze in this way, the lecturer will seem to have spoken directly to every student in the room at least once during the course of the lecture. This may be unnerving for a few, but most students respond very positively to this evidence that their existence is acknowledged.

This use of eye contact is very difficult, however, if the lecturer's presentation consists of reading from a script. So much attention is required of him, in case his place is lost, that there is little opportunity for looking at students. In fact, there is probably little likelihood of any learning either, for nothing is so dull as listening to someone read continuously for fifty minutes. It is eminently preferable to use notes rather than work from a complete lecture script. When a person lectures from notes he may read his key ideas, but is guided by cue words when he elaborates through examples. As mentioned previously, handouts, slides, blackboard summaries or overhead projector transparencies may all be used to present important material, allowing the lecturer freedom to leave his lectern and interact with his students in a more relaxed way.

Bligh (1972) has stated in his review of the research that:
1. Lectures are as effective as other methods for imparting information, but not more so.
2. Lectures are less popular with students than other methods.
3. Lectures are relatively ineffective to stimulate thought.
4. Lectures are relatively ineffective for changing attitudes.

Whether these findings are correct or not, they are generalities. Individual academics can achieve far more using lectures than would be suggested by the rather dismal conclusions listed by Bligh. By employing some of the ideas I have outlined in this chapter, instructors can greatly increase the amount of learning which takes place in lectures. To this end, probably nothing is more important than relinquishing the 50 minutes of monologue and replacing it with a variety of activities emphasizing two-way communication. Such behaviour is likely to keep the lecture method alive and well despite the demands for its abolition.

# Chapter 6

# The productive use of small group discussion

## What is a Small Group Discussion?

Research evidence (Bligh, 1972; Costin, 1972), has suggested that lectures, though likely to be superior in the transmission of information, are less effective than discussion in helping students interpret knowledge, solve problems, think creatively, and change attitudes. In addition, it would appear that students would like more of their teaching to take place in small groups (University Grants Committee, 1964).

If a particular teaching method does not work to the detriment of learning, (and there is no evidence that group discussion does so), and if it is popular with students, there seems a strong case for its extensive use. This may be done by combining it with more formal lecturing to effect increased two-way communication between instructor and students. Ways of achieving this, of creating lecture-discussion sessions, were suggested in the previous chapter. The present chapter looks at discussion conducted in small groups as a teaching method in its own right, examining how it might be used to help students learn.

Certain terms require elaboration. How many participants, for example, comprise a small group? Argyle (1967), has suggested an optimum number of five or six, but under conditions of increased student numbers in colleges and universities, groups of this size would probably not be economic in terms of staff time. On the other hand, once the number of participants approaches eleven or twelve, students become increasingly reticent about venturing an opinion. This defeats the purpose of small group work where it is hoped members will feel free to talk openly and spontaneously, clarifying their ideas and cleaning up the misunderstandings. Full participation by all members of the group is the ideal and, though this may be rarely attained, conditions should be such that the possibility is always there. Accordingly, it would seem preferable to aim at a group size of approximately 5-10, for with this number of participants, there should exist sufficient divergence of opinion to generate useful discussion while still allowing enough "space" for everyone to be heard.

The word "discussion" itself requires clarification. As Combs et.al. (1974), have pointed out, it is easy for people to engage in talk. This doesn't mean they are engaged in group discussion. The purpose of discussion, at least in the educational setting, is to explore and discover personal meaning. Combs draws a distinction between two kinds of group discussion which are used at the tertiary level. One of these is the *decision group,* whose objective is to arrive at a consensus or decision on some issue. Tutorial and seminar groups would usually be categorized in this way because of their task-oriented search for solutions. A second type is the "exploratory" or *"learning group"* in which the objective is not to arrive at decisions, but to help each participant to explore ideas and discover meanings through interaction with other people. These two types of small group discussion are not mutually exclusive, and some form of synthesis would seem to offer the most productive learning environment. Ways in which this synthesis can be achieved will be outlined a little later in this chapter.

In addition to the distinction made above, there are other ways in which small groups may be categorized. Labelling them tutorials or seminars is perhaps the most popular. The term tutorial now means something rather different from the one tutor to one or two students format practised at the English universities of Oxford and Cambridge. Its use has been generalized to describe groups ranging in size from five to twelve which meet together to discuss difficulties arising during lectures, or to consider topics generated by the course controller. The distinction between this and the seminar is somewhat tenuous, but seems to reside in the on-going character of tutorials. Tutorials are normally a systematic series of discussion groups involving prescribed reading and assignments, whereas seminars are likely to be held on a more occasional basis for a specific purpose. They may be more topic-centred than tutorials, and often revolve around the presentation of formal papers prepared by participants. Numbers in seminars may be greater, too, than those normal for tutorials.

The similarities of these two kinds of small group discussions are more important, however, than the rather theoretical differences which are often drawn between them. Both involve a number of students inter-acting in a face to face situation. This implies a certain seating arrangement, with each participant being fully visible to all other participants. A circle is the best way of achieving this situation, though variants in the form of semi-circles, squares and horseshoes are utilized at times to achieve particular objectives. With the seating arrangement facilitating face-to-face interaction, it is easier for individuals to take chances, to offer tentative ideas, partly formed hypotheses, and "off the cuff" reactions which may stimulate the thoughts of others. It allows a student to "stick his neck out" and to make mistakes which can then provide fuel for group discussion. Hopefully, such discussion will provide clarification of half formed ideas, providing opportunities for participants to learn how to learn.

Much depends on the group leader, for he must play a role different from his normal one of authority, the "knower of all truth". Probably his most important function becomes that of reducing the threatening aspects of the situation so that participants feel safe to contribute, even when they are not certain of their correctness. Our insistence on the certainty principle in education has, unfortunately, had an inhibitory influence on our attempts to encourage learning among our students. We learn through trying out things, and if we are condemned for errors, our exploratory behaviour is reduced until no longer will we venture an answer unless we are convinced of its correctness. If a tutor or seminar leader is convinced that there exists a right and a wrong answer to everything, and that his task is to ensure the discussion of right answers only, he is unlikely to promote effective group work. One of his hardest tasks will be increasingly to abdicate his position as leader, to sit back even when he knows the "desirable" answer, and to permit his students to explore ideas for themselves, learning from each other. As we move further into a consideration of group discussion techniques, ways in which the tutor can structure the situation in order to achieve this will become apparent. However, such a change in role is likely to occur only if academics are able to see the values inherent in small group discussion. Although the method is just as capable of abuse as is lecturing, it is likely to embody at least some of the following virtues.

## Virtues of Small Group Discussion

Reasons for using small group discussion as a method of teaching are many and varied. In a survey of five hundred English university teachers, mainly from departments of science, Beard (1970), found that the objective which outweighed all others was to help students clarify difficulties arising from lectures or other teaching sessions. It was a general assumption that small group methods were suitable in this context. A second important reason for its use was the desire to obtain more intimate and personal contact with students than was possible in lectures. Small discussion groups were seen as providing the situation in which this became possible, just as it was seen as facilitating the promotion of critical and logical thinking, aiding problem solving and applications of theory, and giving practice in oral presentation of reports. Many other objectives were mentioned in this survey, closely paralleling the findings of McKeachie (1969a), in the American context. He felt the discussion group to be particularly appropriate when the instructor wants:

- to give students opportunities to formulate principles in their own words and to suggest applications of these principles.
- to help students become aware of and to define problems based on information derived from readings or lectures.
- to gain acceptance for theories or information counter to folklore or previous beliefs of students.
- to get feedback on how well his instructional objectives are being attained.

There is a distinct shift away from the information transmitting function of the lecture towards objectives considered as "higher" by most universities and colleges. Whether they were actually able to achieve such aims or not, higher education authorities have implied that their major objectives do not lie with transmitting information. Rather they lie with teaching students to think in particular ways, with fostering certain attitudes seen as part of the educated man, and, possibly with developing satisfying personal relationships. These things do not seem to be attainable through the use of lectures but are more likely to be achieved in small group discussion.

Abercrombie (1970), has identified the basic rationale for the use of this teaching method when she points out its intention: ". . . to emancipate the student from the authority-dependency relationship, and to help him to develop intellectual independence and maturity through interaction with peers." (p.5). In her own work, Abercrombie has organized group discussions which have helped students to examine their previously unrecognized basic assumptions. Through provision of an environment in which spontaneous conversation relevant to the topic is encouraged, she has focused attention on the interaction between all participants, students and teachers alike. Exposed to the same information as his fellows, each student learns how his interpretations vary and how his biases operate to distort his view of reality. Through such interactions, he learns of his own strengths and weaknesses, and, hopefully, becomes able to modify his attitudes as he sees the wide range of alternatives present in the group. He learns that his "reality", which seems so obvious and so right to him, may not be the reality of any of his fellow participants.

One great virtue, then, of small group discussion is the opportunity it provides for students to learn about themselves and about others, enabling them to work independently and yet co-operatively within a team (UTMU, 1976). Because all participants in a group share the responsibility for its success or failure, they are afforded the opportunity to relinquish dependency on a leader. Every group member may play many roles in a discussion group — initiator, harmonizer, clarifier, evaluator — and by so doing become, at different times, a leader himself. The best groups are those where the leadership function is shared in this way, for participants are permitted to feel their contribution has been of value. This sense of personal enhancement is possible in group discussion to a far greater extent than in the lecture room. As varying roles are adopted, the student has the opportunity to achieve both greater understanding of himself and of his fellow group members. In learning to become more sensitive to the views of others, and to their different ways of thinking, the student can develop a more comprehensive view of his subject and, by doing so, become more enthusiastic about it. If this parallels a growth in self-expression through the practice or oral skills, he has indeed learnt by his experience.

Learning from others is an aspect of particular importance. How often, in the traditional lecture situation, and also in authoritatively run tutorials, do we find students really paying any attention to the contributions of their peers? Their attitude reflects the belief that the "expert" exists to tell them the way things are and that anything their fellow-students might say is unworthy of note. In the small group situation, where the tutor's role as authoritative expert is reduced, students find they can learn from testing their ideas on their peers. They continue to learn from their tutors as well, probably more effectively than in a lecture because of the more informal atmosphere. Overall, the resources available for idea testing are enlarged and enhanced awareness of individual progress is achieved. The feedback to the tutor about the effectiveness of his teaching and to the student about the effectiveness of his learning is facilitated by the small group format (Nuffield Foundation, 1973-5).

Bligh (1972), has pointed out the relative ineffectiveness of lectures in bringing about student attitude change. Group discussion is more likely to achieve this admittedly difficult objective (McLeish et.al. 1973). Reviewing the evidence on the power of the group to influence its participants, these authors conclude that individuals are changed by their experience. The primary mechanism of such change involves the student thinking about what he has said. He worries about the way he has expressed himself, whether his statements had the intended impact, whether he lost face, and so on. Perhaps more important than the discussion itself may be this period between group meetings which allows for the integration of thoughts, a re-assessment of performance, values and roles. As McLeish et.al. have expressed it:

"This is surely the specific virtue of a discussion group compared to the most effective formal presentation by an expert — that it tends to generate reflective thinking because of the deeper personal involvement of the student with the views expressed by himself and his peers." (p.181).

This may be too idealistic a view. Perhaps it is too much responsibility to place upon a teacher. The small group discussion format can permit the achievement of the aims outlined above but whether it does so depends on the leader. As Ottaway (1968), has said, the value of meeting students in small groups depends on at least two general factors, both of which are a function of the instructor's skill:

● The opportunity for a free discussion with full participation by all the members of the group.

● The development of a special type of relationship between the tutor and his students.

If these two factors prevail in a particular group, many advantages are forthcoming by which the needs of both tutor and students may be met.
In brief, these are:

● All have equal rights of participation, to initiate discussion or offer criticism.

- Students are helped to think for themselves, being expected to show their own methods of reasoning.

- Students are enabled to learn from each other, not relying solely on the nominal "expert".

- The tutor can "abdicate" (temporarily), his status as an authority and take on the interpreter or clarifier role. In this way he encourages students to think for themselves and helps them do so more effectively.

- The tutor can encourage "feedback" on students' reactions to the course, helping him identify their learning weaknesses and also assisting him to collect information likely to lead to course improvement.

- The tutor does not always "abdicate". If he has been able to create a warm, permissive atmosphere, his utterances on particular aspects of the topic are likely to be well accepted. As they are relatively few in number, their impact is far greater than under conditions of "minilecturing" when tutors' pronouncements occupy most of the meeting time.

- Students and tutor can establish a personal relationship by face-to-face contact. If love of a subject is caught rather than taught, it would seem the small group provides a most conducive environment for this to occur.

So many advantages attendant on one teaching method would suggest that it is the answer to the problems of higher education. It isn't, of course. No one method is, and the small discussion group has its disadvantages too.

## Problems of Small Group Discussion

The problems involved in small group discussion do not seem to be inherently a function of the method itself. They are more a result of the way it is used. As with lecturing, it is the interaction between teacher and method which generates problems. This is fortunate for it enables us to overcome these problems by trying different approaches. This we could not do if the method itself was at fault.

Some of the most important disadvantages of small group work have been outlined in a paper by Potts (1973). He argues that conventional discussion methods do not provide sufficient space in which participants can express themselves. In a group of one tutor and ten students running for fifty five minutes, each member would have five minutes talking time. With a situation such as this, involving considerable competition for the limited time available, interruptions are the norm with one group member prone to cut across the argument of another participant in order to present his own ideas before the opportunity has passed. The only way such a group can actually work is if a considerable number of its members are silent. Discussion, then, typically involves three or four assertive or well-informed students and the tutor, with the rest of the group playing the part of spectators. These passive students may learn despite their lack of participation. However, through their lack of involvement they deprive other members of additional ideas and insights. By so doing, they inhibit that open discussion which is considered so valuable a part of the small group method.

The tutor may further exacerbate the problem. Unless he is particularly well skilled in group dynamics, he is inclined to dominate the discussion, taking a disproportionate share of the time available to the group. He tends to do this because of his greater knowledge of the subject matter and his desire to direct the proceedings along the "right" path. As a result, discussion tends to be restricted with individual students each talking to the tutor in turn. Little student-to-student interaction takes place in such tutor-dominated sessions and the group usually arrives at the predetermined conclusions. They have done little work themselves to get there. It is the tutor who works hardest.

This is such a prevalent pattern that it might seem unavoidable — an inescapable weakness of a teaching method which looks good on paper but simply doesn't work in practice. It is easy to blame the tutor for permitting it to happen, yet the students are at fault too. If they arrive unprepared, as so often they do, it is easy for the discussion to develop into a "probing of mutual ignorance". Such discussion is often out of focus, rambling, and right off the track. Constantly repeating material already covered is characteristic of sessions where students arrive unprepared, but the number one problem is lack of participation. Threatened by his lack of knowledge and fearful of pressure from the tutor, the student plays safe, volunteering nothing and looking as unobstructive as possible. Unable to evoke any real response, the tutor sees no alternative but to "lecture" with resultant boredom all round.

It is difficult for the tutor to change this pattern if he has no knowledge of the processes involved in the conduct of successful groups. When silences occur, due to his mounting anxiety, he is unable to wait for a student to fill the space but talks on himself. This is natural enough. Students are quick to realize what is happening and will sit back, letting the tutor carry the brunt of the session. Knowledge of his subject is not enough in such situations, yet that is the assumption prevalent in institutions of higher education. No attempt is normally made to ensure tutors have the necessary skills enabling them to facilitate learning in groups. It is assumed anyone can sit down with a group of students and lead an effective discussion. Ignorance that the skills involved are far more critical than in the lecture situation is the main reason why so many discussion groups simply do not work. They do not achieve any of the valuable objectives outlined earlier. Instead, they are a stressful or boring ordeal for student and tutor alike. Fortunately they do not have to be like this, for there are a number of things we may do to improve the functioning of the groups we take. One of these involves the use of subdivision to reduce the threatening aspects of speaking before ten or more group members and to increase the likelihood that everyone will participate.

## Subdividing the Group

Nyberg (1976) has used the term "coagulation" to describe his particular approach to beginning a lecture-discussion course. The whole class, whether it be ten or three hundred and ten is divided into groups of no more than five strangers. No previous acquaintances should be in the same group for, as Nyberg uses it, the method is an acquaintanceship exercise. Each group elects a spokesman. He or she will have the responsibility of introducing the members of the group to the class as a whole. Within the groups, each person has five minutes to inform his fellow members, and particularly the spokesman, about himself in terms of how he would like to be introduced. After each person has been introduced to the group he has the right to amend or rebut the introduction immediately.

Although Nyberg has described this approach in terms of helping students get to know each other at the beginning of a course, it may easily be adapted to the small group situation. In a group of twelve students, three sub-groups of four may be formed to discuss a particular topic. Students who are reluctant to talk in the larger group are not normally so reticent when conversing with only three other people. One of the four participants is elected as leader and after a predetermined time he reports back to the larger group on the main points of the discussion. He attempts to include in his report something said by each member of his sub-group. Thus there are three reports made in which the contribution of each of the twelve students is included.

A similar approach, this time based on written papers, has been described by Lane (1975) under the title *clustering*. Students prepare papers, bring them to class and organize themselves in groups of three. Within these sub-groups, papers are exchanged and read, accompanied by questioning and discussion. Each student then retrieves his own paper, adds any new ideas he may have picked up from the discussion, and hands it into the tutor. This arrangement may be used for small group work where participants number up to twelve or for much larger classes. In this latter case, clusters of three may be formed to read papers and clusters of eight may be formed for discussion purposes. There is a great flexibility in the technique, with clusters forming for specific reasons, objectives and tasks. Some of the more common of these are problem solving, responding to questions, information exchange, interchanging prepared papers, discussing textual problems and evaluating papers and tests. The instructor may sit in on one or several clusters, but his most important task is to collate the material which has been generated. He may do this himself or call on students to say what they have discovered.

Both clustering and coagulation have obvious similarities to the buzz group which was described as a way of improving two-way communication in lectures. Their purpose is to increase participation, through a sub-grouping procedure which reduces the number of students involved in speaking to each other. Although the instructor still plays an important part in organizing the material generated by the student's discussion, greater emphasis is placed upon *peer teaching*. This is one of the great virtues of small group discussion techniques. They permit and encourage students to learn from each other. As Mackenzie et al (1970) have commented: "A student's colleagues often represent the least recognized, least used and possibly the most important of all the resources available to him". Students do seem to learn from each other, often more effectively than from their teachers. Communication is more likely to be at an appropriate level, in terms of language, experience and interests. If students have special skills and knowledge, it seems reasonable to provide opportunities so they may share these with their colleagues. Not only do the recipients benefit from such an interchange, but so too do the "student teachers". We seem to learn best those things we teach to others.

## Dyadic or One-to-One Discussion

Sub-dividing small groups does facilitate peer teaching for there is more opportunity for all to participate. A logical extension of this idea is to reduce numbers even further by having a group of ten to twelve students work in pairs. Working in dyads does overcome most of the problems of small group work outlined earlier in this chapter. One interesting approach to dyadic discussion is that suggested by Potts (1975). He calls his technique one-to-one discussion and it involves students pairing off to talk to each other in turn for specific periods of uninterrupted time on a given question. One member of the dyad asks the question of the other who then has, for example, four minutes in which to formulate an answer. While he does so, he is uninterrupted by his partner who simply listens, encouraging him with non-verbal cues such as an attentive posture and an interested expression. The roles are then reversed, with the listener having his opportunity to answer the question. Assuming the particular question was: "What is motivation?" and the names of the pair of students Joan and

John, the process would look like this:

John: Joan, tell me what is motivation?
Joan: Talks for four minutes uninterrupted giving her ideas on the question, then says: 'John, tell me what is motivation?
John: Talks for four minutes uninterrupted in answering the question.

Once each partner has had his or her period of uninterrupted time, the process may be repeated or else the two students discuss the question back and forth for a further period of time.

Although this idea of time restriction and non-interruption may seem limiting, it does have many advantages. Firstly, the "space" problem of traditional group discussion is overcome with each student able to talk for fifty percent of the time. Some of this time would be guaranteed interruption free and the rest spent in normal give and take discussion. Potts suggests reserving some time at the end of each session for the tutor to put his own viewpoint, so each student would actually have something less than fifty percent of the time available for speaking. Still, he has the opportunity to participate far more than in the conventional small group format.

Not only does this one-to-one discussion method encourage greatly increased student participation, it also overcomes the problem of tutor dominance. Though he may take part in the interaction as a member of a dyad, the tutor has no prescribed role as a talker or a listener. By setting up the dyadic situation, he actually creates opportunities for discussion without predetermining or anticipating student responses. He poses questions, suggests readings, and present himself as an ideas source to the group as a whole, or through particpating himself in the one-to-one discussion.

A third advantage of this method lies in the generally high quality of the discussion generated. This would seem to be a function of the long stretches of uninterrupted time (four or five minutes can seem a very long time under these conditions) which imposes some pressure on the speaker to organise his thoughts coherently. He normally finds it harder to talk aimlessly than to develop a theme and explore it rationally. Further, it could be claimed that people argue most irrationally when they are frequently denied and interrupted. To counter such occurrences, they resort to overstatements in order to seize attention and space. Such behaviour is unnecessary when talking space is protected as it is in one-to-one discussion.

Enhanced personal relationships are a final important advantage of this approach. Partners change frequently so that each member of the group meets other students in quite an intense way. This is true not only of student-to-student interaction, but also if the tutor takes part in the dyadic discussion, of student-to-tutor interaction. People get to know each other well as they talk to each other, and the whole group can achieve a high degree of cohesiveness in which learning becomes a pleasurable activity.

In his learning cell approach, Goldschmid (1971) also makes use of dyadic discussion although the structures he uses are a little different from those of Potts. Students still interact in pairs, the partners changing after each one hour session. Two alternate procedures for using these cells are suggested. The first of these is applicable when both members of the dyad have been set the same assignment. Students carefully read this assignment on their own and prepare, before the next group meeting, a number of questions relating to the text. Some of the questioning possibilities could well be an inquiry into the main points raised by the reading, the content of other readings or course materials related to the assignment, and the relationships between the content of the assignment and student's relevant personal experiences. It is often helpful for students to provide the tutor with a carbon copy of the questions they intend to ask their partner. This is not only a check on their preparation, but is also a source of feedback on how the method is working. It is interesting to note that lack of preparation usually ceases to be a problem under conditions of dyadic interaction. Students, who may have no compunction about lack of preparation for a conventional tutorial, feel they would be letting down their fellow students if they engaged in one-to-one discussion without the necessary background.

Once the session gets under way, the questioning pattern, which does not have the time limits of the Potts' approach, is:

John: asks his first question
Joan: responds to this question
John: elaborates or corrects if necessary
Joan: asks her first question
John: responds to this question
Joan: elaborates or corrects if necessary

Possibly the tutor will reserve time for himself at the beginning or end of the session or both to present his viewpoint and clarify difficult ideas. As the dyads interact, he may rotate from one pair to another giving feedback, asking and answering questions and evaluating students' performance. Alternatively, the tutor may prefer to leave the students completely alone.

Where reading lists are long, Goldschmid suggests a second procedure whereby each member of the dyad prepares different material. The emphasis in this case is not upon the reviewing of material as in the first procedure, but upon the learning of new knowledge, with one member of a dyad teaching the other. The pattern here is:

John: describes the main points of his material and asks his first question to check
    Joan's understanding
Joan: responds to the question
John: elaborates and corrects if necessary: asks his next question
Joan: responds to the question

This pattern continues until the half-way point in the session when the two members of the dyad reverse roles with Joan teaching her material to John.

There exists some experimental validation of this learning cell approach, indicating its superiority to traditional discussion groups, seminars and essay methods of teaching (Goldschmid, 1970; Goldschmid & Shore, 1974), and to problem solving on an individual basis (Alexander, et al, 1974). The reasons for the superiority of such peer-assisted learning would seem to be:

1.  the active practice of subject matter with attendant feedback for immediate evaluation
2.  increased student motivation due to enjoyment derived from students studying together
3.  students' development of responsibility for their own learning and for that of their partner
4.  provision of an effective environment for learning how to learn.

The particular dyadic discussion approaches which have so far been described envisage an entire teaching period of fifty to fifty five minutes being used for peer interaction with perhaps a short time reserved for tutor comment. This is one way of using the method. Another is to combine it with discussion in the larger group. If this pattern is used, the first half of a teaching period might be used for one-to-one interaction while, during the second half, all students come together to consider the ideas which have been generated. The great advantage of this approach lies in its combination of the virtues of both dyadic discussion and small group discussion. Participation by all members is virtually assured by the one-to-one, and the building of group cohesiveness is encouraged by the later pooling of information. My own experience (Stanton, 1977a), has indicated that students will talk far more readily and far more intelligently when general group discussion is preceded by dyadic interaction. Students are able to try out their ideas on their partner, clarify their thoughts and revise first impressions. They then feel more confident in expressing themselves in the small group situation.

I would carry this point further, suggesting that tutors should commence their courses with a one-to-one format. When a tutor first meets his group at the beginning of an academic year, it may take considerable time for the "ice to be broken." Often, such a thawing never occurs, and a stiff, distrustful group of people go through the entire year deriving little benefit from their tutorial sessions. Having students pair-off with someone they don't know, discussing questions such as "Tell me something about yourself?", and "How do you expect your work this year to contribute to your enjoyment of life?", very quickly establishes strong bonds. After such one-to-one discussion, when he moves back into the larger group, a student may then introduce his partner to other members. Group cohesion develops rapidly when the first session or two is devoted to such acquaintanceship activities, preferably with the tutor mixing himself in with his students. Although there may be some initial anxiety about the procedure, this usually disappears very quickly. To some, using one or two sessions in this way would seem a waste of time which should be devoted to the academic task. It isn't. Building a warm group atmosphere in which participants can feel sufficiently comfortable with each other to speak freely will facilitate group discussion. It is one way of combating the main obstacle to successful small group work, the lack of participation. There are numerous other ways, too, of coping with this problem.

## Increasing Participation of Group Members

An essential basis for useful discussion is a common informational basis. Usually we attempt to achieve this by setting work to be done before the group meeting, perhaps in the form of reading, preparing a paper or working a problem. The difficulty with such an approach is students' reluctance to prepare themselves in this way. Session after session may fail because of such unpreparedness, yet, other than bemoaning the laziness of students, we continue on in the same way, finally concluding that small group discussion methods are useless. This need not be so. A solution is to provide a common informational base at the commencement of the session. This may take the form of a short handout, a video tape, film, an overhead projector transparency, a 35 mm slide, a chart showing experimental data, or anything else designed to stimulate interest and provide information. By beginning a session in this way, the tutor ensures that everyone taking part in the discussion will be talking about the same material. Because the information is fresh in their minds, students are more ready to participate. Their chances of saying something pertinent and helpful is enhanced just as the chances of an embarrassingly incorrect comment are reduced.

Abercrombie (1969) has provided an excellent example of this approach in her work with medical students. Seminars would begin with about twenty minutes' individual work on a provocative and relevent task such as a study of two x-ray photographs. Working alone, students would compare these, making a list of the differences they observed. This would be followed by an hour's discussion in groups of 8 - 12, the tutor remaining relatively silent while students discussed their findings. Interventions by Abercrombie centred on the assumptions being made, the way interpretations were being regarded as observable facts. By making explicit these hidden assumptions, Abercrombie helped students to "see" things in new ways and to sharpen their observational and reasoning powers.

Beginning a small group discussion well is very important. Provision of a starting stimulus helps create the conditions under which active student participation can take place. Attention to the seating pattern can also contribute. Assuming group members are seated in a circle facing each other, it is useful to seat very dominant students beside each other and not facing the tutor. Opposite such students place quiet members who normally participate little. Organizing seating in this way will help achieve the aim of encouraging the participation of all students, for most interaction in small groups is across the circle. Voluble students will tend to speak to those sitting opposite, providing the stimulation required to provoke a response from these normally reticent members. This is why I suggest the tutor sits across from quiet students. By verbal and non-verbal cues, he can bring them into the discussion. Unless the intention is to instigate hot debate between dominant students, do not seat them opposite each other, for all other members of the group will be then forced into the position of onlookers.

Once the discussion is underway, stimulated by an interest provoking opening, there are various actions the group leader may take to keep the participation level high. Usually these involve a reduction of his own role from that of dominator to a more subtle one of stimulation based on careful listening. If the tutor glances around the group, for example, while a student is speaking, he reduces the pressure, for he no longer fixes him with the inquisitorial eye. It also helps to keep other students attentive to the speaker. The speaker, in turn, is encouraged to follow the tutor's example, letting his eyes rove around the group while he talks. This tends to promote more student-to-student interaction rather than student-to-tutor-to-another-student type discussion.

The tutor's questioning techniques are important, too, for misuse can effectively stifle participation on the part of students. Asking questions which have only one right answer, known already to the instructor, is an example of such misuse. More open ended questions are of greater value, particularly those drawing on students' own experience in a concrete way. Knowing something of a student's background can be very helpful here and such knowledge may be readily gained through the use of the acquaintanceship sessions suggested earlier. Controversy may be stimulated, too, through drawing on such information in the form of questions designed to bring out differing viewpoints. As such controversy begins, the tutor moves back, metaphorically, allowing other group members to interact freely with each other.

An early statement of opinion should be avoided by the tutor, particularly if it is couched in terms of great assurance. Students need encouragement to challenge the ideas of others, particularly when delivered by one in authority and a permissive approach is more likely to be successful in achieving this end. When a student asks a question of the tutor, he may turn it back with "Well, what is your opinion about this?" or redirect it to other group members with "Has anyone else ideas about this?" The tutor is a model, and his behaviour, rather than what he says, will influence the degree of participation he rouses amongst his students. It is useless for the tutor to say he wants everyone to participate freely if his own actions indicate his lack of appreciation of students' efforts. Wrong answers, for example, need not be critically rejected, but may be used as starting points for developing more correct responses. The student might be asked to explain further or other group members requested to give their opinions.

Reward is normally more effective in shaping behaviour than is punishment (Skinner 1968). Good answers, good questions and general participative behaviour can be encouraged verbally with a word or two indicating recognition. "A good point." "Well put, John." "An interesting viewpoint, Sue," and non-verbally with a smile or nod. Use of a student's name is helpful in encouraging freer participation. So, too, is attentive listening as an opinion is expounded. Conducting a small group discussion in this way requires sensitivity on the part of the tutor and attention to what is happening in his group. By allowing his eyes to move constantly over the students, the tutor will often obviate the need to intervene verbally. As one participant comes towards the end of what he is saying, the tutor can usually observe various non-verbal signals indicating the readiness of another student to contribute. These may take the form of an intake of breath, a shift in seating position or a glance towards the tutor. Their recognition enables the tutor to "bring in" the student with a hand gesture, a look, or a lifted eyebrow.

The blackboard can also be of help in facilitating participation, particularly where an argument over a point is developing. Such conflicts are part of any good discussion (McKeachie, 1969a), but should not be left ambiguous and uncertain. Focusing of the group's attention on the blackboard as key points are written up helps them clarify their ideas on the contentious issues. Maier's (1963) two-column method is a useful model. One column is headed "Favourable to A" and the other "Favourable to B" where two opposing viewpoints are concerned. When a single view has been proposed, the columns may be labelled "For" and "Against". As participants speak, their contribution is noted appropriately on the blackboard. Everything is recorded at this stage. Once the basic material has been gathered in this way, a second stage commences with areas of agreement and disagreement being considered, alternatives evaluated, and some sort of resolution attempted.

This approach has similarities with *brainstorming* which is even more flexible in accommodating everything group members may wish to contribute. A question is asked, a problem posed and students are requested to provide as many ideas as possible relating to the issue. Anything, no matter how odd or seemingly impossible, is accepted. Students are encouraged to be creative, to let their minds free-wheel beyond normal limits and solutions. In this idea generation stage, judgment is suspended for no attempt is made to evaluate the worth of the contributions. Once the creative faucet runs dry, then the ideas are considered more critically, attempting to sort out those likely to provide the best answers to the question, the best solutions to the problem. Brainstorming encourages wide participation because of its temporary suspension of evaluation and is helpful in the creation of a vital group atmosphere.

An alternative approach, serving the same purpose, is Delbecq and Van de Ven's (1971)*nominal group technique*. It is reputed to generate a higher quality, quantity and variety of ideas than brainstorming which is seen to suffer from the disadvantage of group members tending to react to their peers' ideas rather than concentrating on developing their own. In its first stage, the nominal group technique sees students spending ten minutes writing down individually, and without interaction with others, as many answers as possible to a question. Once this task has been completed, the tutor acts as recorder, noting the answers on the blackboard as they are read out to him. No discussion is allowed at this second stage, answers being recorded without interpretation or argument. A third stage involves discussion, with each idea on the board being clarified and considered carefully as to its implications. Selection comprises the fourth stage. Each student lists, in order of priority, the ten points he considers to be "best", and then, in the final stage, engages in further discussion to arrive at some consensus based on these lists. As with brainstorming, a key feature is separation of the processes of idea generation and idea evaluation. If such separation is permitted by a tutor, he should find students far more prepared to contribute and "risk" themselves than they would in a more traditional situation.

Another key feature of both brainstorming and the nominal group is the summing up of earlier discussion. It is important for tutors to either provide such clarification themselves or encourage group members to do so. This provides a sense of direction and should be directly related to the task upon which the group is engaged. Unless this is done, a sense of aimlessness can pervade the discussions which take place. Feelings of futility ensue which, if allowed to persist, will dampen the most enthusiastic of participants. The process is really one of ensuring that all students know what the group is trying to achieve and relating ongoing activities to this objective. Such summarizing, from time to time, reminds the group of its progress and of its unfulfilled commitments. However, not only is it important to monitor the groups' progress towards its task goal, it is also helpful to consider the actual process in which it is engaged. How is it coping with its task? Is the discussion productive? Are students engaged in the experience and learning from their participation? These are all process questions which really determine the group's success or failure.

## Improving Group Processes

A tutor is normally chosen for his subject matter competence, and he conceives his task to be that of achieving certain academic goals. Anything occurring in his group not directly related to that objective is considered irrelevent. On the surface this seems an eminently reasonable approach. The surface agenda, the task to be achieved and its related sub-tasks, is surely enough to worry about. Unfortunately, it is the activities going on below the surface which make or break a group. Napier & Gershenfeld (1973), after reviewing many studies of groups in action, make this point succinctly:

"If members spend their time strictly with business — the surface agenda — and ignore interpersonal relationships and hidden agendas, misunderstandings can increase and communication is limited . . . However there is evidence that if the group spends more time initially in permitting people to discuss their personal goals and to get to know each other, they build a common frame of reference, a "set towards problem solving," (p 119).

This is a rationale for acquaintanceship sessions, but the implication of hidden agendas goes further than that. If students are helped to feel more comfortable with each other and encouraged to express their feeling about the group activity, obstacles dealing with the surface agenda may be more quickly removed. Dimock (1970) has affirmed that ". . . it is more often the hidden agendas and unexpressed feelings that block the group coming to a decision than the actual differences in stated content." (p 28). When a block occurs with no progress being made towards its solution, it is time to bring out the unexpressed feelings and deal with them. Is Judy bored? Does Bob resent the dominance of Graeme? Has Bill turned off? Unless these issues are dealt with openly, various group members simply drop out and make no contribution. An interesting exercise, when things have bogged down, is to have students write down their thoughts at that particular moment. Often only a very small number will be thinking about the surface agenda. They will be busy with hidden agendas related to

59

their own personal goals and feelings. As long as these remain concealed, little progress is likely to be made towards achieving the academic task goals. When these unexpressed feelings are brought out into the open and resolved, the group can benefit from the experience for they are learning something about how they operate as people and how they operate as a group.

Therefore, it is worthwhile to pause periodically and examine how a group is progressing, both in terms of its academic task and its cohesiveness. This latter term may be used as an umbrella to cover variables such as a student's enjoyment in being part of the group, his willingness to participate, his eagerness to initiate activities and his level of co-operation. The basic questions to ask are: "What is going on here? How do we feel now, at this moment, about what we're doing? Are we in trouble? What can we do about it?" Opening up group processes for study in this way contributes to cohesiveness and enhances problem solving effectiveness. Every group member can be helped to feel part of a process greater than himself and to feel that his contribution to the group's health is important. Responsibility for success is vested not only in a tutor, it is shared by all participants if the group is to be successful.

Actually it is often helpful to provide a situation in which students can learn more about the way in which groups function. Again, the cry of "wasting precious time which should be spent on attaining academic objectives," is likely to be raised, and quite legitimately so. Yet, according to the experience of hundreds of lecturers and tutors in many higher education institutions, small group discussions just do not work well. Students "vote with their feet" and stay away. When they do come, achievement of objectives is often minimal. Both tutor and those students who remain are bored. It would seem that any action likely to produce improvement here would actually facilitate the attainment of academic objectives, by helping the group process to operate more effectively.

One way of doing this is to use a process observer. He may be a member of the group itself, (a different one each time the technique is used), or an outside advisor, perhaps from a Staff Development and Advisory Unit. Such a person takes no part in the group discussion, but simply observes what is happening, asking himself questions such as: "Are group goals clearly understood? How is discussion focussed? To what extent do members participate? Is hostility and aggression among members apparent? Is the group moving towards its stated goals? Does the tutor's behaviour facilitate learning? Is he helping the group work as a group?" The process observer may also map group interaction, diagrammatically recording the direction and frequency of participants' contributions. This material is all fed back to the group at various points during the session, or at the next session so that efforts may be made to effect improvements.

The use of audiotape or videotape further enhances the likelihood that such observation can lead to behaviour change and an improvement in group functioning. Dominant speakers, for example, rarely realize the extent to which they interrupt others and hold the floor for long periods of time. Non-participants rarely realize how their non-verbal cues, such as yawnings, shuffling, looking bored, can dampen group activity. Through a discussion of process, such students can be helped to face up to their responsibilities. If someone is bored in a group discussion, it is up to him to do something about it. It is not the responsibility of other people to help him out unless the boredom is general. In this case, the tutor will have to do something about it. For the individual, it is up to him to say: "Look, I'm bored with this discussion. It's getting nowhere. Let's get on to something else." If he does this, he will soon find out if he is with the group or the odd man out. Others may agree, and, as a result of the frank statement, the group goes off on a new direction, hopefully more productive. On the other hand, other participants may disagree. If this is so, the fault would seem to lie with the bored student and it is his responsibility to get into the ongoing discussion.

He can be helped to do so by practice in role playing. In any group there are many different roles. Kilby (1974) has categorized these in this way:

- Group task roles — (a) initiator and contributor (b) information seeker (c) opinion giver (d) elaborator.

- Group building and maintenance roles — (a) encourager (b) harmonizer (c) standard setter (d) expediter.

- Individual roles — (a) recognition seeker (b) special interest pleader (c) self-confessor (d) dominator.

With a list such as this before them, students are asked to select the three roles they usually play in general and in the present group in particular. After fifteen minutes of silent evaluation, each student talks about the roles he chose and why he feels the need to play those roles. The rest of the group then provides feedback on whether they see him in the way he has just described himself. The exercise can be extended by conducting a group discussion with members deliberately choosing to play roles different from the ones normally adopted. One session spent in this way will often lead to great improvement in subsequent group functioning.

Whether a group can function with this degree of openness depends on the climate created. This is, initially, the responsibility of the tutor and through the use of some of the methods outlined in this chapter, he should find it possible to create a warm, encouraging atmosphere in which students will feel free to fully participate. Such an environment has been frequently linked with improved learning (eg. McKeachie & Kulick, 1975; Rogers, 1969; UTMU, 1976). It also makes higher education a more pleasant experience for both students and teachers. It may not be the whole answer to improving the group discussion method but it goes a long way towards achieving that aim.

# Chapter 7

# Facilitating learning through individualizing instruction

## Independence in Learning

Mountford (1966) expresses an oft-repeated theme when he sees the aims of a University as encouraging students to ". . . be receptive to what is new, eager to explore it, show ability to cope with it and — above all — to be able to work confidently on their own." The desirability of students learning to think and work independently has been echoed by tertiary institutions other than universities, yet examination of higher educational practices suggests that relatively little has been done to transform the desire into reality. It would be very difficult for anyone but the most biased of observers to claim that the fostering of independence is the central aim of most academics. Study of higher education courses and assessment methods show little evidence that the capacity for independent study and thinking is rewarded to any significant extent (Beard, 1970). Instead, the emphasis would seem to fall heavily upon the memorization of information provided by the lecturer which is then returned, preferably intact, at examination time. Many academics may not say that this is their aim. Rather, they will stress the more intellectually respectful objective of independent thinking. However, the truth lies in their behaviour as reflected in courses, teaching techniques, and assessment methods, not in the words they use to describe their behaviour.

To some extent, this is not entirely the fault of lecturers. Students entering higher education come from tightly structured learning situations and expect to encounter somewhat the same in their new environment. Such expectations can exert a powerful influence on lecturers who find it easier to act as information transmitters than to establish the conditions under which students have to do much of their own learning. This does not necessarily mean turning them loose with no guidance — although this has been done on occasions. The more normal pattern has been to replace classroom attendance with a variety of alternatives such as reading, self-generated projects, and guided study so that the student is given increased autonomy to pace his own learning and to follow, within limits, his own learning inclinations. In contrast with traditional lecture-tutorial systems, the physical presence of an instructor may not be required at all (e.g. Milton, 1973, Stanton 1974a). If the lecturer does play some more active part, it is normally as an advisor-guide rather than as an authoritative information dispenser (e.g. Goldman et al., 1974; Stanton, 1975a).

Basically, such approaches provide students with a clear statement of objectives, a reading list specifically designed to assist in the achievement of these objectives, reference to or provision of other resources, sample test questions, and a date for completion. These assignments, or learning packages, vary in duration, covering a week, a month or a semester. The actual degree of independence granted to students varies. Rarely is there complete freedom from time restraint. Students are usually given the opportunity to work when they please provided certain pre-determined tasks are completed by set dates.

Similarly, the choice allowed in the selection of favoured learning modes may differ. Variations in the degree of freedom allowed can range from a direct choice between lectures and reading to the situation where only objectives are given, with students deciding for themselves the resources they require and the appropriate strategies they should adopt (Mager & Clark, 1969). Options may be provided, too, as far as choice of content is concerned. Themes for projects and essays may be selected entirely by the student, or by a conference between student and course controller. The actual course curriculum may be set without student involvement or they may be permitted to modify it in accordance with their particular interests. Only one particular sample of content may be provided or many alternatives may be given, allowing students to choose their own path. The same range of choices applies to assessment methods.

It is difficult therefore, to precisely define independent learning other than to point to the greater freedom enjoyed by students to move away from strict instructor control of pace, mode and content of learning. Some degree of responsibility for their own learning is granted to students, the amount varying according to the instructor's willingness to modify the degree of control he exerts. Instead of "the" resource, he becomes one resource among several. Rather than remaining as the "teacher", he becomes more the manager of a learning environment, organizing his course in a way which he feels will help students learn more readily. He becomes, in short, a facilitator of learning.

Often he fails. His trust in the ability of his students is not confirmed. They do not avail themselves of the opportunity to learn for themselves, despite the best of intentions (e.g. Goldman et al., 1974). Deprived of the rigidly structured lecture situation, they do not seem sufficiently motivated to engage in the learning tasks. Perhaps we start too late. Where independent study seems most frequently to fail is when ". . . . there has been a sudden imposition of the demand that a student function with a high degree of intellectual independence for which he has had no reasonable preparation. To allow a student to spend the first two years of college in highly structured classes . . . . and then . . . . to turn him loose to engage in independent study is to court the disaster that many independent study projects report." (Raushenbush, 1967. p. 198).

The implication of this view is clear. Begin training students to work independently as soon as they commence their higher education, before they lose their zest and enthusiasm through becoming bogged down with formal course work. What research evidence we have (e.g. McKeachie, 1960) suggests that students are capable of undertaking independent study in their first year, and such experience does seem likely to produce honours and post-graduate students more competent in learning for themselves. This is an assumption though, for there exists no substantial empirical support for such a view. Independent study is no panacae, for as McKeachie points out, we still know little about the types of students, teachers, previous training and objectives necessary for its success. Despite this, we can help students make a success of independent study by; discussing fully with them the new kinds of expectations and demands they are likely to meet, and providing an on-going consultative service; using students with more experience in independent study courses to give assistance; making available instruction in the particular study techniques required; and providing a "safety net" in the form of a structured course if students are unable to cope with the more ambiguous learning situation. This last point refers back to an idea expressed earlier, that it is desirable to teach courses in a number of different ways so students may have a choice of learning modes.

In an attempt to overcome some of the problems associated with independent study, there has been, in recent years, a strong movement towards Individualized Instruction Systems. Such systems are usually highly structured, resolving the ambiguity of more free-wheeling programmes, yet do provide students with freedom to learn more independently than they would under the lecture-tutorial system. They attempt to:

- Cater for individual learning styles, usually by permitting variation in learning rate, choice of instructional media, and freedom in choice of working time and place.

- Actively involve the student in the learning process.

- Use criteria-referenced assessment, with a student's progress being defined in terms of his mastery of set objectives, rather than in terms of comparisons with fellow students.

To achieve these aims, an individualized instructional system requires three characteristics:

1. It must have explicitly stated behavioural objectives which provide reference criteria.

2. It must provide the student with a rapid and efficient means of assessing his or her progress.

3. It should facilitate two-way interaction between the student and the teacher.

Possibly the best known of these systems is that devised by Keller (1967, 1968) and generally known by the title of Personalized System of Instruction.

## Personalized System of Instruction (PSI)

As Keller has explained it, the distinguishing features of his approach are:

- The go-at-your-own-pace feature which permits a student to move through the course at a speed he finds comfortable in terms of his own ability and the other demands made upon his time.

- The unit-perfection requirement for advance which permits a student to move on to new material only after he has demonstrated a mastery of that which preceeded it. Mastery is defined in terms of gaining 100% on unit tests, though failure to achieve this level is not penalized. Students are permitted to re-learn and take additional tests until they attain the 100% criteria, at which point they move on to the next unit.

- The course materials are divided into sufficiently small units to permit such complete mastery, with objectives of each unit being specified in behavioural terms. That is, it is specified what students have to be able to do at the end of each unit. To solve a quadratic equation, is an example of such a specification. To distinguish between psychological theories on the basis of certain criteria, is another.

- The use of lectures and demonstrations as motivating techniques, rather than as sources of information. Information is normally supplied by study guides which include the specific objectives and suggestions as to how their mastery might be achieved (for example, by reading certain pages of a textbook, by listening to a particular audiotape, or by viewing a set of slides).

● The stress placed upon the written word in teacher-student communication with study guides and tests replacing oral classroom interaction.

● The use of proctors, which permits repeated testing, immediate scoring, almost unavoidable tutoring and a marked enhancement of the person-social aspect of the educational process as the result of each test is discussed individually with the student.

A high premium is thus placed on a principle already discussed, that of rewarding or reinforcing desired responses. When students learn as reflected in their gaining 100% mastery on a test — they are rewarded both through praise and the knowledge of their own achievement. (Some developers of PSI systems have used a less strict criteria of 90%, or even 80% mastery). Proponents of PSI avoid the unpleasant, threatening or aversive learning conditions which often prevail in other approaches to university and education. For the Keller Plan is a teaching method and specifically designed for higher education, initially in the area of psychology, but since expanded to many other disciplines such as physics (Green, 1971), biochemistry (Welsman & Shapiro, 1973) and mathematics (Smythe, 1974).

Peer teaching is another previously mentioned principle which plays an important part in Keller's approach. His application of it in the form of proctoring is highly structured. Students who have previously taken and done well in a course are placed in teaching roles and given course credit for assisting in this way. Proctors provide students taking the course with study materials, give and score written tests, and discuss with each student his results. Originally Keller used graduate students as proctors, but found them unsatisfactory because of their tendency to mimic the instructor and lecture rather than just give feedback to students on an individual basis. His solution was the "advanced" student as described above. However, certainly within the Australian higher education context and, I suspect, that of many other countries, such an arrangement is unlikely to be very practical.

A more viable alternative might be the assigned-peer proctor system described by Tosti (1973) which chooses proctors from among the "better" students taking the course. They are each responsible for a group of fellow students, numbering ten to fifteen, this number remaining constant throughout the course. A variant of this approach is to have the proctor "on duty" at certain times during the week. The "duty' proctors do not have assigned groups, but serve anyone who attends during their duty time. Identification of "better" students normally involves the lecturer grading the first fifteen or twenty unit tests and asking for volunteers from those who have done best. Apparently, according to Tosti, recruiting is no problem, even when proctors are not rewarded with credit hours, bonus points, or payment. Most students find the proctoring role rewarding, this possibly being a function of an enhanced sense of personal worth. Perhaps it is also related to a point made earlier, that a person seems to learn more through teaching than through being taught. Experimental evidence confirming the academic gains of peer teachers is derived mainly from the school setting (e.g.Gartner et. al. 1971; Thiagarajan, 1973) but seems capable of generalization to higher eduction.

A problem with the system outlined above is the demands made on the proctor's time. This may be overcome by using a rotating peer-proctor system. In this case, the first group of students through each unit is evaluated by the course controller and asked if they would like to be proctors. This process is repeated after every unit so that a proctor's duties last for only one unit at a time.

Experimental data on PSI is generally favourable, with examination performance usually equalling and often exceeding performance from lecture courses (e.g. Van der Klauw and Plomp, 1974). This finding seems to hold for slow learners, that is, those who need to repeat many tests before attaining the mastery criterion, as well as the fast learners who need only one test each unit (Whitehurst, and Madigan, 1975). Although he did not collect comparative test data, Green (1971) reported his experience with PSI in a physics course in highly favourable terms. His conclusion was based on ratings of teaching staff, student performance tests, and student questionnaire responses.

As far as the lecturer is concerned, the most obvious result of conducting a course along the lines suggested by Keller is that he no longer occupies the centre of the educational stage. He has prepared the necessary material, enshrined it in study guides, and may, if he wishes, play the role of tutor. It is highly desirable for him to do this, particularly while the course is in its infancy, so that he may learn something of the difficulties that students are experiencing. Occasionally, he may still function in a more traditional role by giving a motivational lecture, but this often becomes a rather disappointing experience. When lectures are optional and not related to examinable material — unless the instructor has something of real value to give — he is unlikely to attract many students. To them, course success is a function of mastering unit material, and lectures are often seen as irrelevant. Much as we may bemoan such an attitude, it seems to be the reality of the situation. Students focus on specifically defined objectives and direct their activities towards achieving them, just as they try to do under other teaching methods. Because such objectives are clearly outlined with PSI, this behaviour becomes more obvious. Perhaps, then, such an approach is spoonfeeding?

Not so, according to students. Responses to questionnaires attempting to evaluate their reactions to PSI courses have generally indicated quite the contrary. Most students seem to work harder than under lecture-tutorial conditions and use their time more efficiently. Lectures are seen as the real spoonfeeding rather than PSI courses which give freedom to work within the broad framework provided by the units (Sherman, 1971, 1972). Some of the features of PSI accepted by students as particularly valuable, such as performance objectives, self-pacing and frequent feedback, are also seen in modular instruction, another attempt to systematize independent learning.

## Modular Instruction

A module has been defined by Goldschmid and Goldschmid (1973) as: ". . . a curriculum package designed for self study. It is a self-contained, independent instructional unit which may be combined with other such units to form . . . a planned series of learning activities designed to help the student accomplish certain well defined objectives." Modules may be used in a variety of ways, ranging from the insertion of one of two into a traditional course, through to complete courses which consist of a prescribed sequence of modules and courses that offer students choices of a certain number of modules from a larger array (Creager and Murray, 1971).

The purpose of such an approach is to provide for student variability. They have a choice of pace, setting their own rates; a choice of learning mode, for modules include a wide variety of learning activities such as viewing audio-visual media, participating in projects, performing experiments and reading textbooks; and a choice of topics. Flexibility is built into modular instruction whereby students, though experiencing frequent evaluation, are able to change pace, mode and topics, to achieve more effectively the stated objectives. A student begins a module by taking a test to determine if he or she has the necessary prerequisite knowledge and skills. If such prerequisites are lacking, some form of remedial instruction may be provided. On the other hand, a student may reveal he already has competence in the knowledge and skills to be taught by a particular module and so is directed to study at a more advanced level. Thus students are not made to learn material for which they are unready or material which is already known to them.

Generalizing this idea, it would be a salutatory exercise for lecturers to test students on the contents of their own lectures before they presented them. On occasions they would discover such a paucity of prerequisite knowledge that to proceed would be a waste of time. Conversely, on other occasions, they would find their classes had no need of the lecture because they already knew the material to be covered. Fortunately or unfortunately, depending on one's viewpoint, lecturers are protected from such traumatic information by their reticence in finding out what actual state of readiness their students have attained. Feedback, as has been noted, is noticeably lacking in the formal lecture situation.

When a module is completed, students are tested again and allowed to proceed if the objectives have been attained. Failure at this point means some form of recycling through remedial modules, repetition, or a change of learning mode. Such immediate and continuous feedback, providing information to the student on how much and how well he has learned and to the instructor on how effective his "teaching" really has been, is only one of the advantages claimed for modular instruction.

Many others appear in the following chart (adapted from Postlethwait and Russell, 1971) which presents a summary of the differences between conventional and modular instruction.

| Characteristic | Conventional Course | Modular Course |
| --- | --- | --- |
| Course Success | Mostly judged subjectively by the instructor | Objectives and evaluation assure that the instructor is able to correct faulty instructional materials and knows when his course is successful in terms of student learning. |
| Instructional Activities | Mostly lectures and written assignments; media used on basis of instructor's personal feelings about them | Many different instructional activities are used to optimize learning; media used on basis of efficacy established through trial use by students |
| Learning Experience | Oriented toward teacher performance, with emphasis on teaching | Oriented toward student performance and individual instruction, with emphasis on learning |

| | | |
|---|---|---|
| Mastery | It is expected that only a few students will do very well and some will fail | Given enough time, all students are expected to achieve mastery of the objectives |
| Objectives | Usually not stated in precise observable terms | Stated in terms of student behaviour and presented before instruction begins |
| Participation | Passive | Active |
| Presentation of Materials | Group-oriented at pre-determined times | Highly individualized, each student can use any or all of the instructional materials, available at preferred times |
| Rate (or pacing) | Students must all go at the same rate | Each student can proceed at his own rate |
| Reinforcement | Usually only after major examinations | Immediate and frequent, after small units of material studied |
| Role of Instructor | Disseminator of information | Diagnostician, prescriber, motivator and resource person |
| Test References | Norm-referenced tests are used ("grading on a curve") | Criterion-referenced tests are used; success is independent of performance of fellow students |
| Testing | Student typically takes one or two tests (sampling the material "covered") which determine his grade for the entire course | Designed to measure mastery of the objectives stated at the beginning of the course; purposes are assessment of pre-requisite skills; diagnosis of strengths, weaknesses and mastery |

Virtually any course has some component or components which may be presented in modular form. Although most of the disciplines using this approach have been in the general area of science or social science (see Goldschmid and Goldschmid, 1973), the arts and humanities need not be excluded. Despite the tendency to rely on vague generalities — often found in these discipline areas — it is possible to formulate more precisely their objectives (Stanton, 1972d). Not all aspects of a course may be so defined, but that is not really an argument against the use of modules. Whole courses do not have to be treated by the same approach. Modules may be used where appropriate, perhaps once or twice in a course where they seem most likely to achieve the desired learning objectives. Other aspects of the course would be taught in other ways. This is the essential flexibility of the approach where, even within a particular module, a student has a choice — a choice between objectives, materials and learning modes. The permutations are endless.

Design of instructional modules consists of a series of basic steps. Haefele (1969) has suggested one such approach to the development of a self-instructional package.

1. Prepare a comprehensive list of broad objectives, embracing general concepts, understandings and principles.
2. Translate these into specific behavioural objectives, specifying what students should be able to do by the time they complete the module. Action verbs such as define, identify, solve, are useful at this point. In addition to objectives, prerequisite behaviours needed should be outlined.
3. Establish peformance standards and criterion levels. For example, "Identify at least three sources of error . . ."
4. Arrange the learning activities such as grade sheets, films and slides, needed for mastery of the objectives.
5. Use headings such as that given below to organize the module.

   ● Broad objectives
   ● Behaviouralized specific objectives
   ● Prerequisite objectives or tasks
   ● Learning activity
   ● Performance criteria

Goldschmid and Goldschmid (1973) would see module development a little differently. Their step-by-step sequence would read like this:

1. State a minimum number of objectives in behavioural terms. (Identifying specific topics to be taught will probably precede this step).
2. Organize these in a hierarchy which determines the sequence of instruction.
3. Design a pre-test to diagnose students' competencies on starting the module.
4. State a rationale for the module, indicating its value to the student.
5. Design instructional activities to help students achieve the objectives. Provision of options is important.
6. Design a post-test to measure student achievement or otherwise of the objectives.
7. Provide a resource centre where all readings and materials necessary to complete the modules are made available.

The authors of this approach do provide some experimental evidence for its effectiveness, although very little research has been done in the area. They sound an optimistic note however, echoing the conclusion of one investigation (McDonald & Dodge, 1971) that modular instruction "seems to fit the needs of a large number of students and provides for them the avenues of learning which are founded upon success, not failure". That was, of course, Skinner's (1958) guiding principle when he proposed the use of programmed instruction, the forerunner of all the present individualized instructional systems.

## Programmed Instruction

Emphasis, in programmed instruction, is upon success. It is based upon carefully sequenced series of statements designed to elicit correct responses from the student. Because the progression from one statement or "frame" to the next is so gradual, the likelihood of error is minimized. Thus, when the student fills in this written response, his chances of being reinforced through giving a correct answer is high. The programme, which consists of the sequence of frames, is usually presented in book format, and the student works through this at his own pace, his speed depending on the facility with which he arrives at correct responses.

Linear programmes are the more common, primarily because they are easier to write. Students work through the frames in a pre-determined order, normally following all the steps included in the entire unit. Occasionally a remedial series of frames is inserted to provide additional assistance for a student who answers a test frame incorrectly, or provision is made to allow a student to skip a sequence of frames if his answer to a previous question indicates his possession of the knowledge contained therein. Although this more flexible format is rarely found in linear programmes, it is the essential feature of those called "branching" programmes (Crowder, 1964). In this case students read a test frame which has a number of alternative answers printed below. Depending on their choice of response they are directed to appropriate pages of a book which either congratulates them for a correct answer and sends them onto the next frame, or explains why they were incorrect and redirects them back to the original question for another attempt. Frames in branching programmes are usually larger than those of the linear type where one tiny piece of information is added to that which was conveyed in the previous frame.

Pressey (1963), the originator of the first teaching machine in the 1920's, has moved away from reliance on either of these two formats, suggesting a more flexible approach which he labels "adjunct autoinstruction". Where orthodox programming arbitrarily fragments subject matter into many small frames, each with feedback, Pressey has claimed that the length and nature of a frame should vary according to objectives, materials and student competence. It might, therefore, vary from a single sentence to an entire chapter in a book. Also, he sees feedback as occurring only when needed, not as a necessary part of every frame. Because of this flexibility, Pressey has suggested adjunct programming as particularly suitable for facilitating learning in an independent study context. Students could, for example, study a textbook chapter and then answer a series of multiple choice questions based on the key points they had read. Such self-testing would guide them as to the effectiveness of their learning.

The criticisms levelled against orthodox programming by Pressey, and his suggested alternatives of using programmes as adjuncts to lectures and reading, point up the main reason for its relative lack of success in higher education. Programmed instruction is generally rather boring, particularly in its usual linear form. Learning step by step with tiny increments of knowledge prevents students seeing the overall picture. They see the trees but may miss the forest! Particularly at universities and colleges, students presumably have the cognitive skills to cope with a general overview and then fill in the component parts. Basically this reflects the conflict of theories between the behaviorists and the cognitive-field adherents as to how learning takes place. As my own bias lies in the latter direction, I believe learning is a matter of seeing relationships and finding significant personal meaning in the information presented. Linear programming does not lend itself to such cognitive operations. The branching format is more helpful, but as such programmes take an inordinate amount of time to write, very few of them are used in higher education.

Programmed instruction does seem as effective as more conventional methods in terms of test results, and often courses are covered more quickly (Beard & Bligh, 1971). This is probably due to the clarity with which instructional objectives are specified and the opportunity students have to set their own pace. However, this approach has not led to the revolution in teaching methodology that its supporters expected, for students generally seem to prefer conventional texts. The message which does seem to emerge clearly from the experimental work is that programming is best used as part of a system of instruction, rather than as a means of teaching an entire course. Where programmes concentrate on teaching essential information in 'skeleton' form, they can be an effective means of facilitating student learning (Beard & Bligh, 1971). For lecturers wishing to use programmes in this way, information concerning their availability has been provided by Cavanagh & Jones (1969) and Hendershot (1971). Most of these are in printed form, but programmes may be presented aurally by means of audiotape or visually by means of videotapes, films and 35 mm slides or both aurally and visually. Postlethwaite's (1971) audio-tutorial system for biology students at Purdue University is a well known example, and reflects a trend to conduct science laboratory sessions in ways more likely to encourage independent learning.

## Individualized Instruction in Practical Sessions

Postlethwaite's intention was to create a laboratory environment conducive to active student involvement and to this end he centred his instruction around the audio-tutorial carrel. Seated in this carrel, or booth, a student listened to a programmed audio-tape which directed him through a number of learning activities. Unlike the printed programmes outlined in the previous section, these audio-tapes involved students in a variety of activities including lectures, reading, examining visual materials, studying specimens, doing experiments and watching films. Although students are able to work through the programme at their own pace, the study carrels being available most of the time, they do have a clear structure guiding their progress. As Postlethwaite has described it, emphasis on teaching mechanisms has been replaced by a concern for student learning. The audio-tutorial approach:

" . . . involves the teacher identifying as clearly as possible those responses, attitudes, concepts, ideas and manipulatory skills to be achieved by the student and then designing a multi-faceted, multi-sensory approach which will enable the student to direct his own activity to attain these objectives. The programme of learning is organized in such a way that students can proceed at their own pace, filling in the gaps in their background information and omitting the portions of the programme which they have covered at some previous time."

This approach is only one among many which mark a definite trend away from didactic instruction in science practical sessions towards learning by discovery. At Sydney University, for example, Brewer (1977) has used Postlethwaite's self-instructional module approach, modifying it to include interactive groups. In this way, students derive benefits both from independent study and from discussion with their peers and tutors.

Quite a different concept is reflected in The Open University's Technological Foundation course where students design, build, load and test a load-bearing structure using balsa wood which is later subjected to competitive destruction tests (UTMU, 1976). This is seen as a viable alternate strategy to that of using established pieces of equipment, particularly as students gain practical experience in checking compatibility of materials, resolution of forces, analysis of structure and aesthetics.

The standard experiment repeated year after year, and the standard laboratory report written up in terms of how things should have turned out (whether they did or not) is, at times, giving way to more open ended activities, or project-type experiments. Students are often brought together in both large and small groups to present and defend their experimental data, defending it against arguments from other students. In such cases, the "right" experimental findings are not pre-determined, and discussion is encouraged on the variability of the data produced. If

71

such discussion is conducted on very open lines without the leader using his authoritative position to spell out the accepted answer, students are enabled to see their practical work as something more than a boring rehash of a field which has already been heavily worked over (Smythe, 1974).

Project type experiments may arise from such free discussion. Although used in many fields other than the sciences, projects generated by an individual or by a group of students provide another variant on teacher dominated practical sessions. According to the University of London's Teaching Methods Unit (1976), projects commonly have the following characteristics:

- They involve the solution of a problem. Often, though not necessarily set by the student himself.

- They involve initiative by the student or group of students, and necessitate a variety of educational activities. These activities are usually the responsibility of the student though guidance is available from tutors or demonstrators.

- They result in an end product. For example, Christopherson (1967) has suggested that engineering laboratory reports could take the form of a consultant's report to the lecturer acting as a client, or a commercial brochure describing the operating and advantages of a particular piece of equipment.

- Work often goes on for a considerable length of time, ranging from a single afternoon to several years. If the latter is the case, care must be taken to ensure students have appropriate sub-goals established, for long term goals are often very ineffective motivators. Having something to aim at which is capable of achievement in the near future is more likely to sustain persistent effort.

- Teaching staff are involved in an advisory rather than a didactic role at all stages — initiation, conduct and conclusion.

The project method stresses independence of activity. The student is responsible for making decisions about his own learning, but should have a supportive group and tutor-demonstrator to turn to when he needs additional help. It is of prime importance, however, for the student to be actively involved in the choice of project rather than have it decided for him, and to explore for himself the attendant constraints. It is one thing to decide on a series of experiments designed to contribute to a particular result; it is something else to actually translate the decision into a practical plan. The learning involved in attempting to do so may be more valuable than the results produced, and it is here that the tutor-demonstrator must allow the student considerable freedom. As pointed out earlier, he may not use this freedom wisely.

It is understandable that students left alone with little guidance may be unable to handle the responsibility of independent learning. That is why structured individualized instruction has become of importance. At various times over recent years, programmed instruction, PSI, and modular instruction, have all been hailed as the answer to the ills of higher education. Theoretically, these structured approaches seem very sound, impressive in their meticulous planning and careful monitoring of student progress. They provide a learning environment in which students are given a share of responsibility for their own learning, without having to relinquish the support offered by a clear structure. Yet, I don't believe that the face of higher education will be changed by this means. Development of courses based on structured individualized learning principles requires a great amount of time and effort. Lecturing is easier and less time consuming and, human nature being what it is, lecturing is likely to remain a far more popular activity than designing learning packages. Time spent in meticulous course design is rarely rewarded. We would be better advised to devote more energy to our research and publication if we desire academic advancement. So human laziness and lack of reward are powerful forces working against the *widespread* use of Individualized Instructional Systems. Despite this, their use will continue to grow in some higher education institutions and by so doing provide another educational alternative. As a greater variety of learning opportunities is provided, pressure is put on practitioners of the traditional lecture method to improve their performance. Perhaps, in this way a general improvement in the quality of higher education will be effected.

# Chapter 8

# The value of Educational Technology

In this chapter, we will consider two ways in which educational technology may prove of assistance to the lecturer who wishes to facilitate the learning of his students. The first of these involves the design of courses which actually achieve what the lecturer wants them to achieve. Though we assume that students are learning those things we intend them to learn, we may be mistaken, as Corey (1949), has pointed out:

"The best way to find out what college students are learning is to observe what they are doing. If they spend a great deal of time reading and discussing Great Books, they are learning primarily how to read and discuss Great Books. They are not necessarliy learning how to behave in harmony with the principles elucidated in Great Books. If students in science classes spend most of their time in laboratories following detailed instructions that appear in a laboratory manual, they are learning better how to follow detailed directions that appear in a laboratory manual. They are not necessarily learning how to apply the scientific method of thought in situations that are to them new ones . . . If students in a college get a great deal of practice following the directions which members of the faculty give them, these students primarily are learning better how to follow the directions given to them by members of the faculty. They are not learning to be resourceful and to stand on their own feet." (p.28).

Corey's comment is very pertinent to the issue of independent learning raised in the last chapter. Students will not normally work well on an independent basis until they learn how to do so, and we need to establish the conditions under which such learning will take place. His comment also focuses on a reason why so many of our courses are ineffective. We assume what we are doing will produce certain results. Often it doesn't, but as we lack feedback on how students actually perceive our offerings, we are unaware that this is the case. Thus, we continue conducting our courses the same way, year in, year out, assuming we are achieving our aims, not realizing students are learning quite different things from those we intended. Educational technology can help us improve upon this situation, for it " . . . embodies one crucial value — that it is a good thing to say as clearly as possible what it is you are trying to do, how and why you propose to do it, and in what manner you will judge the effectiveness of the system you thereby create." (Rowntree, 1974. p.11).

Helping us design courses with greater precision is one contribution of educational technology. A second, which is part of this concept of systematic course development, is the guidance provided in the effective use of audio-visual media. Rather than being something added on to embellish a lecture, almost as an afterthought, media is seen as part of a carefully organized learning experience designed to achieve a particular aim (Hall, 1977c). When such an approach is adopted, the effectiveness of media use may be evaluated along with other elements involved in the system.

## Systematic Course Design

Educational technology really revolves around the idea of objectives. As Mager (1962) put it: "If you're not sure where you're going, you're liable to end up someplace else — and not even know it." It is important to know where we are going in any course we design, not only because it provides a goal at which our teaching may be aimed, but also because it allows us to measure how effective we have been. With objectives as a starting point, the basic steps involved in curriculum planning are:

1. Define the objectives of the course, preferably in terms of what things students should be able to do at the end that they were unable to do at the beginning.

2. Consider the alternative learning experiences available by which students could be helped to achieve these objectives. Audio-visual media would be involved at this point, with decisions being made about its appropriateness for bringing about the particular learning outcomes envisaged.

3. Select the most promising alternatives and expose students to them.

4. Assess students at various points as the course proceeds to gauge the success of the particular learning experiences. At the completion of the course, match student attainment with objectives to get an overall measure of its success.

5. Use the results of this evaluation to modify other components in the "system". Perhaps the learning experiences provided were not completely successful. Additions or deletions could be contemplated. Perhaps some of the objectives were unrealistic and could be improved in the light of staff and students' experience with the course.

The process is one of give-and-take flexibility. There should be provision for change within the course to increase its effectiveness as measured by students' success in attainment of the objectives. Despite the linear format in which the five steps have been set down, there is constant interplay between them. Though it is useful to define objectives early in the planning sequence, it is inevitable that we need to come back and redefine them as we consider the alternative learning experiences and our evaluative instruments.

The whole exercise may be seen in terms of problem-solving (Rowntree, 1974). Student attainment of academic course objectives is the problem, and various hypotheses are proposed as likely means of solving the problem. The alternative hypotheses are translated into concrete learning experiences and are tried out on students whose relative success or lack of success is then measured. These measures provide the basic data feedback enabling hypotheses to be modified until the problem is satisfactorily solved. At this point, a lecturer could well feel that he has a good course.

The same procedure is also applicable to individual lectures and tutorials. Hopefully, each of us enters a classroom with some idea of what changes we hope to induce in our students. The purpose of education is to effect change (e.g. Rowntree, 1974), but our problem often lies in our own lack of clarity about such change. We are uncertain about what we are actually attempting to achieve and adoption of the more systematic approach outlined above will help us avoid such vagueness. Once we are clear about our aims or objectives, it is important to let our students in on the secret; for I believe we have no right to change other people without first letting them know what we are attempting. Co-operative planning is not only indicated on these moral grounds, it is also conducive to more effective learning (Wight, 1972). Based on the systematic approach described, the student might well use a guide such as the following:

- Where am I going? (objectives)
- How do I get there? (learning experiences)
- How do I know I am making progress? (assessment against short term objectives)
- How do I know when I have arrived? (assessment against end-of-course objectives)

Courses designed in the way suggested above provide constant feedback for staff and students alike, who feel the motivation generated through knowing where they are going. Students benefit, too, from knowing how they are to be assessed, for the criteria are clearly spelt out. They have certain specified objectives to attain and they will be assessed on whether they have attained them or not. This procedure is a corrective to one of the educational malpractices described by Stewart (1971):

> "In addition to the variability among teachers on the criteria used for grading essays, students are not informed as to what these criteria are . . . if students are told what the criteria are, then most students will achieve what they are supposed to, and teachers can't end up with a 'satisfactory' grading curve. *According to our present educational philosophy, it is better not to let the students know what they are* supposed to learn because they are liable to learn it." (p.26).

Such secrecy about criteria is no part of the approach recommended by the educational technologists, who place a premium on clarity. Vagueness and lack of direction are seen as the great sins of higher education. It is possible, however, to go too far in the other direction, becoming so obsessed with spelling out objectives that the task involved becomes too great. Designing courses is a time-consuming business, and specification of minutely detailed objectives so adds to this burden that the whole concept of the educational technologists is rejected. This is rather a case of throwing out the baby with the bathwater, for most of us would, I think, accept the idea that systematic course planning is likely to assist students learning. What is not so readily acceptable is the necessity to define objectives precisely.

## The Role of Objectives or Aims

Eisner (1967) has objected to the use of specifically stated behavioural objectives on several grounds, the most important of them being that:

- the outcomes of instruction are often unpredictable, and therefore not all outcomes can be specified in advance;

- different types of subject matter place constraints upon objectives so that, in Arts subjects for example, it is difficult to specify with precision the particular operation or behaviour the student is to perform after instruction;

- quantitative evaluation is often inappropriate, as when an aesthetic object is produced, for it is qualitative judgement that is then required, not the use of an educational objective as a standard of measurement;

- specification of objectives initially as a guide to curriculum planning is logical, but not necessarily most psychologically efficient.

The basic objection to the use of objectives which surfaces repeatedly is the feeling that the instructor will be so blinkered by them that he will miss opportunities for fruitful teaching in other directions (e.g. Atkin, 1969). An associated point is that only the most trivial of goals can be specified in any precise way, thus a concentration on such objectives misses all the really important things in education. The relative merits of objectives can thus be argued back and forth ad infinitum, but the really important point seems to be continually missed in such debate. Objectives are a tool capable of use or misuse depending on the person using them. True, not all the outcomes of instruction are predictable, but this does not seem to be a compelling argument against clarifying those outcomes which are predictable. Some of the products of teaching in the Arts subjects may defy specification but not all of them, and perhaps many considered beyond such treatment are not so. For example:

"When presented with two previously unseen prose passages, the student should be able to make a value judgement, choosing one of the two as being more in accord with the accepted principles of English language usage. He should further demonstrate his knowledge of the techniques involved in making such a reasoned judgement by writing an explanation of the basis upon which the decision was made." (Stanton, 1972d. P.52).

Ebel (1964) has argued strongly against the view, often expressed by teachers of subjects in the Humanities, that certain educational outcomes are important but unmeasurable. He would claim that to be judged as important, an outcome of education must make an observable difference in the behaviour of persons who have attained different degrees of it. Therefore, it is measurable. If the attainment of an alleged goal of education does not change, in some way, the overt behaviour of the person who attains it, how can it be described as important? This is the key issue consistently overlooked by opponents of the behavioural objectives approach. Instead they seem to set up a straw man, concentrating their attacks on ways this educational tool may be misused.

Some course designers may be rigidly inflexible and write pages of highly specific objectives which preclude teachers from doing anything else but concentrating on measurable trivia. Others may begin with such objectives and refuse to modify them in the light of later experience with differing content and differing student reactions. They are, I feel, a very small minority. Most people are far more flexible than this and can see value in the intelligent use of objectives whereby general goals are translated into observable behaviour. A pious hope such as: "The student will be able to appreciate experimental method" is not very much help in the design of learning experiences intended to bring about this result. Better to transform this vague idea into something specific which actually indicates what behaviour is expected of the student. Hall & Cannon (1975) do so in the following statement:

As a result of this course it is hoped the student will be able
  — to manipulate pieces of laboratory equipment
  — to recognise when an adequate result has been obtained
  — to discover errors and be able to correct them
  — to evaluate the accuracy of the experiment

Through expressing his objectives in this manner, the teacher knows what experiences he must provide and how he may assess his students to discover if they have been successful. The students know exactly what is expected of them and how they will be assessed. Objectives may be used wisely to achieve such positive outcomes or unwisely to trivialize the whole educational process. It depends on who is using them.

In this section I have used terms such as "objective", "behavioural objective" and "aims" almost interchangeably. This was deliberate for, as the terms are used by different writers, there often appears little difference between them. What distinctions do appear are usually the result of distortions and exaggerations whereby extreme examples are used to establish a case. I have used "objectives" in the sense of intended ways in which students should be different at the end of a course than they were at the beginning. Such differences must be in terms of changed behaviour, otherwise they are unobservable and we cannot claim that any change has taken place. The change may be reflected in increased knowledge, demonstrated verbally or in writing; improved skills, demonstrated in a practical situation; or changed attitudes, revealed by a more energetic approach to a subject. It does not seem useful for claims of increased knowledge or understanding to be made without any attempt to specify what evidence will be accepted that such a change has taken place. Such evidence will be, of necessity, behavioural. The person who understands a concept now which he failed to understand before he took the course will be able to do such things as: put it in his own words, apply it to a new situation, and teach it to someone else. By such behaviour, he demonstrates his understanding. This is what my use of the term "objectives" implies, but I feel that "aims" would be equally as useful. Whatever we may choose to call them, through their use we can help students to learn more readily. We can also do so through using audio-visual media effectively and it is to a consideration of ways in which this might be done that we now turn.

## The Place of Audio-Visual Media

No longer can audio-visual media be dismissed as an appendage, an aid to learning which is peripheral to the real task of teaching. Films, videotape, audiotape and slide series now carry much of the actual subject matter content of instruction and must be integrated as an essential part of the learning experiences provided for the student. Where learning objectives are well defined, the task of selecting appropriate media is relatively uncomplicated. Two criteria may be used to guide such a choice.

Firstly, it is necessary to ask whether the use of media will help students achieve the particular objective involved. If the answer is "no", the inquiry ceases. Media should not be used for the sake of using it. Unless it has a definite function to perform, it has no place in a systematically designed plan. If the answer is "yes", a second question is asked. "Which particular audio visual material is most likely to achieve the desired end?" In a historical context, where the student is attempting to analyze an original document in terms of the valid and invalid inferences which might be drawn from it, the printed word would seem most appropriate (Rowntree, 1974). The printed word would be, however, inappropriate in a situation where the student's task involved distinguishing between mineral specimens. The real thing, specimens, would be required to facilitate the attainment of this objective. Abercrombie (1969) used X-ray photographs with her medical students as the media necessary to help them distinguish fact from inference. In each of these cases, the media used, whether printed word, mineral specimen, or X-ray photograph, was an essential part of the learning experience without which the objective could not have been attained. Yet, we often ignore the assistance which media can give, choosing to rely on words, either spoken or written, to carry the message.

Media selected as appropriate for a particular purpose can be very valuable in improving the communication process in the classroom. Often this process is seen in deceptively simple terms. A teacher on course transmits a message to his students, the target. Diagrammatically it looks like this:

This is the one-way communication pattern so typical of higher education classrooms in which students either receive no opportunity to participate or are too inhibited to do so if given the opportunity. Part of their difficulty lies in the almost exclusively verbal mode of presentation employed by many tertiary teachers. Implicit in such an approach is the assumption that whatever the lecturer says will be correctly interpreted by his students, that his words will mean the same things to them as they do to him. Our own experience would suggest otherwise, as evidenced by the prevalence of student "howlers" which are related with great gusto in faculty common rooms. Often students do misinterpret what we say because their experience is different from our own. They may derive a different meaning from our words than the one we intended. This creates a feeling of uncertainty among students, a doubt that they really understand what the lecturer is explaining. Accordingly, when called upon to answer a question, they hesitate, unwilling to take the chance of appearing foolish through having misinterpreted what is being asked of them. Visuals can improve this position and facilitate the creation of a genuine two-way communication pattern.

## The Use of Visuals

Visuals make a presentation more concrete, and this is particularly important if a lecturer wishes to use an inductive approach in his teaching. Students could be presented with a 35 mm. slide, a film, or a video tape, and be asked initially to simply observe the material. Once this had been done, the next step would involve them describing what they had seen. Because of the visual stimulus used, response is usually uninhibited by doubts over misinterpretation and misunderstanding. Finally, students are asked to explain what they have observed. The lecturer may assist at this point, offering information where gaps are left or errors creep in. With such an approach students' participation is actively sought, based on the use of visuals to facilitate their involvement. The communication model now becomes:

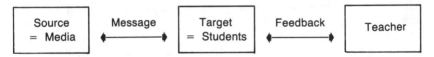

Visuals not only facilitate two-way communication through making student response easier. They also make presentations more interesting. Without visuals, a lecturer's message presentation can become very stereotyped — explanation, perhaps some blackboard notes, and student notemaking. Add to this the variety of overhead transparencies, 35 mm. slides, charts, flat pictures and film, and such stereotyping becomes much less likely. Not that we would use all these materials in any one session. It would be, again, a matter of choosing those which served the particular purpose of the lecture or tutorial.

This purpose may not, however, necessarily be related only to academic work. The geography lecturer may use 35 mm. slides because they are the best available substitute for the real thing, but he may also use them to increase interest among his students. This seems a legitimate rationale for the use of media, for interest is easier to maintain when students' concentration is not directed to the same point for long periods of time. Use of visuals transfers attention from the lecturer to the screen, giving him a chance to remain silent and remove the stimulus of his voice for a while. Changing the light level in the lecture room achieves the same purpose through an alteration in the stimulus pattern. Our geography lecturer who uses explanation, questions based on slides, written work stimulated by these visuals and recapitulation by means of an overhead projector is likely to find the retaining of student interest easier than if he relied solely on his voice and the blackboard. He is also likely to facilitate student learning for it has been estimated that, for most people, up to 80% of our information input comes through our eyes (Coburn, 1968). A combination of sight and hearing is considered to be the most effective way of presenting material in order to enhance its retention, so the combination of visuals with verbal explanation is indicated.

## Audiotape can be helpful too.

Visuals, then, can be useful in helping to achieve our course aims. So too can aural materials such as radio broadcasts, records and tape recordings. The latter are particularly useful, especially since the advent of the cassette, for they can now be made as readily accessible as are books. Instructors may record their lectures and store them in the library. This allows students who have been absent to catch up on material they have missed and permits a re-hearing for students who had difficulties during the lecture itself. Making a recording of one's own lecture is, also, a salutary experience in terms of self-improvement. We can learn a lot from listening to ourselves in action.

Recordings may provide examples during the course of a lecture. An extract from a speech or news commentary, a piece of music or a poem read by the poet himself may serve the same function as a 35 mm. slide used to illustrate a particular point being made by the lecturer.

The tape recorder also provides an alternative means of providing assignment feedback. Instead of returning assignments with his remarks written on them, the tutor may record his comments as he reads the paper. Students supply a cassette as they submit their work and have it returned with the tutor's comments after correction. Student reaction has been quite favourable to this approach, mainly because the comments provided in this way are more helpful as a guide to improving their work. Conversely, students could submit tapes where they talked about their assignment as an alternative to a written explanation.

As mentioned earlier, tapes play an important part in the audio tutorial method of teaching where the student, in his learning carrel, interacts with taped lectures and instructions about using visual and printed materials. Another popular media mix, along similar lines, is the tape-slide programme. An ordinary audio-tape carries a recorded commentary on one track while the other track carries electronic signals which trip the slide-change mechanism of an automatic slide projector at the appropriate moments. The "3M sound-on-slide" system achieves the same effect with less effort on the part of the person preparing the presentation. Such use of media is particularly helpful for skill learning, as, for example, in science courses where the manipulation of basic apparatus is important.

Many of the ways in which individual audio-visual media may be used have been spelled out in books devoted exclusively to this subject (e.g. Brown et al; 1977,

Coppen, 1969; Unwin, 1969; Wittich & Schuller, 1973) so no further elaboration will be attempted at this point. Instead, attention will be focused upon audio-visual materials in general, with emphasis falling upon some of the principles governing their effectiveness in higher education.

## Using Media to best effect

Perhaps the most important of these relates to a point made earlier, that media is more likely to achieve the purpose for which it is intended if it is closely integrated into the teaching-learning process. A four step approach, applicable particularly to the use of film and tape, will normally achieve this end.

1. The first of these steps involves *lecturer preparation*. Films, videotapes and slide series should be previewed before use; audiotapes should be pre-heard. This is not only a familiarization process but a check to ensure that the particular media chosen will actually contribute to the attainment of the instructional objective. Perhaps only certain parts may be of value, or the decision may be made that, in terms of what it can do to facilitate class learning, the media is not worth using. Assuming this is not the case, step two would follow.

2. *Preparation of the class* is necessary to engender a "mental set" so students' attention is directed to the aspects of the media considered by the teacher to be important. Such direction may take the form of a pre-film discussion, the listing of questions on the blackboard or an assignment involving material to be presented by the film or tape. The purpose of such preparation is to let the class know why they are being exposed to the media and to provide a frame of reference within which the material communicated becomes meaningful.

3. Step three is the actual *presentation* by means of the media. Although lengthy notetaking is not recommended at this stage, due to the distraction of attention involved, key points relating to the preliminary discussion may be jotted down. If the lecturer does require a lot of material to be recorded during the presentation stage, it is helpful for him to divide the class into groups, each one being responsible for noting specific information.

4. A *follow up* after the presentation is necessary to ensure students have actually derived the information from the media which was expected of them. Checking answers to questions, discussion of important points and completion of an assignment are ways in which this may be accomplished.

A fifth step may be added if time is available. This involves a representation of the media. When a videotape or film is the media being used, it may be helpful to switch off the sound for this second run through, either superimposing a commentary of your own or having students provide relevant comments in answer to your questioning. Conversely, perhaps only the sound track could be played with students attempting to recall the visual stimuli which accompanied particular parts of the commentary.

## Properties and types of media

If an approach such as that outlined above is adopted, the lecturer will be able to maximize the general advantages inherent in audio-visual media. These are at least three in number (Gerlach & Ely, 1971). Firstly, they possess a fixative property which permits the capture, preservation and reconstitution of objects and events. Once a photograph has been made or an event recorded on film or tape, the information has been "saved" and is available for later reproduction. A second property could be described as manipulative in that objects and events may be transformed in many ways. Time lapse photography enables the speeding up of a process such as the birth of a chicken, while the slow-motion camera facilitates close analysis of skilled performance. Editing of tape and film is easy, permitting material from man sources to be combined and re-combined in new presentations. Thirdly, media has a distributive property. It may be transported through space so that many people can see or hear the same thing at the same time, and this experience may be repeated again and again should it be necessary. An important speech or a dramatic event, such as man's first landing on the moon, can be reproduced in almost any location at almost any time.

Not all types of media necessarily share these three properties, for they vary in different ways. One useful classification indicating this variety has been provided by Henderson (1969):

| | | |
|---|---|---|
| TALK——— | Inter-com — P. A. Systems — Telephone<br>Radio — Recorder — Language Laboratory | ———LISTEN |
| WRITE——— | Books — Periodicals — Chalkboard<br>Paper — Typewriters — Duplicators | ———READ |
| SHOW——— | Movie & Film-Strip Projectors — Teaching<br>Machines — Television — Videotape — Opaque<br>& Overhead Projector — Microfilm —<br>Micro-Projector — Slides — Camera —<br>Photograph | ———LOOK |
| MAKE——— | Maps — Globes — Charts — Paintings —<br>Drawings — Sculpture — Models | ———USE |
| HANDLE——— | Laboratory Equipment — Construct<br>Materials — Tools | ———STORE |

Such a classification provides guidance for the instructor in that it sensitizes him to the diversity of audio-visual materials available. That such media can be effective in promoting learning has been repeatedly affirmed by decades of research (e.g. Flood-Page, 1976; McKeachie, 1969a) but this in itself is not enough. The way audio-visual materials are handled by the individual lecturer himself is vital, for the most valuable of media, if misused, may be actually detrimental to student learning. One possible way of avoiding this has been suggested in this chapter. It is the use of educational technology with its emphasis on clarity of objectives, careful matching of learning experiences (which includes audio-visual materials), and continual assessment of student progress. Through using this approach we are more likely to help our students achieve the things we want them to achieve. If we eschew systematic planning in favour of relying on vague hopes that everything will probably be all right, it is most unlikely that our courses will turn out very well. Preparation and planning are necessary for success in most ventures. Teaching would seem to be no exception.

# Chapter 9

# Have we helped our students learn?

## *Learning — whose responsibility?*

I have defined good teaching as the facilitation of learning, and the good teacher as he who helps his students learn. This view is not without support. In his review of the American literature on the use of student evaluation of teaching, Flood-Page (1974) has commented ". . . . the good teacher to them (the students) is someone who says and does things in the classroom in ways that enable them to learn well". (p.62). Some of the ways to which students refer have been outlined in earlier chapters. However, once the teacher has attempted to put these into practice, he requires information on his effectiveness, on his degree of success in facilitating student learning. He needs to know whether he has been able to pass on knowledge and whether gains in learning have occurred. Unless such data is available, no basis for self-improvement is provided. As Tyler (1959) has observed: "Hence, the development of a sound body of guiding concepts and principles in teaching is largely dependent upon means for evaluating teaching so that our principles have been tested rather than resting upon personal preference, or upon unsystematic impression."

Teachers learn about their classroom effectiveness both from what their students do and what they say. Perhaps the ultimate measure of teaching is that of student performance at end of course examinations. Such a measure has a certain validity, for achievement tests, if they are well designed, show whether students have gained new knowledge and acquired new skills. Thus, they assess students. They also evaluate teachers, for if examinations produce little evidence that students have learned, the implication is that they may have been badly taught. It is not uncommon for a course to produce a failure rate of 30, 40 or 50 per cent. Are so many students unintelligent, lazy and disinterested? Is it entirely their fault they have failed to attain the course objectives, or is the fault shared by their teacher who has not helped them learn?

Rowntree (1974) sees this issue of responsibility as confusing the whole issue of evaluation, assessment and grading. "Who is on trial," he asks, "the teacher or the student? If the student 'fails' his course has he really failed it or has it failed him?" (p.134). It is rare for instructors to put their teaching methods on trial, for they act in terms of intuitive protectiveness. If their students do well, they congratulate themselves on their efforts; if they do poorly, it is due to the students' inferior intelligence, lack of motivation or some such fatal flaw. It is the concentration on grading — sorting students into categories — which is at the root of the problem, for such assessment provides no useful feedback likely to help a lecturer teach more effectively. This is where Rowntree makes a useful distinction between assessment and evaluation. The former is concerned with finding out how the students' abilities and knowledge have changed as a result of the learning experiences to which he has been exposed. The latter is an attempt to identify and explain the effects (and

83

effectiveness) of the teaching. Thus assessment focusses upon the student and what he has achieved in the course. It can provide useful feedback if it can be separated from the grading function and then considered as evidence pertinent to the issue of how well students have learned. If tests and examinations reveal a high percentage of students attaining course objectives, the teacher's choice of learning experiences is confirmed. His methods have been successful. If they reveal a low percentage of students attaining course objectives, remedial action is indicated in the form of course modification.

Evaluation can be very effective at this point for it focusses on the teaching process itself. Assessment is more concerned with the *product* of teaching, whereas evaluation involves student reaction to the teaching *process.* What students do is reflected in their examination results, the course product, but this does not tell the whole story about a teacher's effectiveness. Many factors other than the effects of an individual teacher influence a student's results. Some of these would include the tone of the university or college he attends, the influence exerted upon him by peers and parents, the physical conditions under which he studies, his degree of persistence, and his physical and emotional state on the day of the examination.

What students *say* is also pertinent to the course *process* and this information can be of great benefit to the teacher attempting to evaluate how effective his course has been (Hall, 1977a). Many of us receive informal, casual feedback from students which is relevant to the course we are conducting but, due to its random, probably unrepresentative nature, it is unlikely to provide the basis for the evaluation we desire. Systematically measured student opinion is more informative, producing a wide spectrum of data which tends to balance extreme opinions. A number of rating scales attempting to perform this task of systematic measurement have been produced (e.g. Flood-Page, 1974; Miller, 1972), and these enable teachers to learn how students feel about their courses and their teaching. In the next section, the use of such student questionnaires will be considered in more detail.

## The Evaluation of Teaching

Although attention has usually been focussed on students as the main source of information on course and lecturer evaluation, heads of departments and colleagues have also been considered. Falk & Dow (1971) suggest that evaluation by colleagues in the same discipline is likely to be more reliable than that of students. This is due both to colleagues' greater knowledge of the field being taught and to the likelihood of their agreement on the important objectives of instruction. However, Hildebrand (1972) points out that it is a rare academic department which has ever discussed the criteria for making judgements about teaching effectiveness. Further, most faculty members, including departmental heads, never attend classes conducted by a colleague so their opinions about his teaching are based largely on an unsystematized, informal and usually inadequate sampling of student opinion.

These two divergent views are capable of synthesis. Potentially, colleagues do provide a most valuable source of information which would enable a lecturer to improve his course. In actuality, they don't, because they rarely discuss course objectives and teaching methods, and make no effort to observe colleagues in their classes. This seems a waste of an excellent learning opportunity, for, just as students learn well from each other, so too do teachers. Yet, we remain in splendid isolation in our lecture rooms, masters of our own domains, and deprived of a useful means of self-improvement. Colleagues are very much under-used. Asking one to sit in on your lecture to act as an observer may not only help you, in terms of the feedback you receive, but may help him, too. He might start thinking about teaching in a different way. If such visitations are coupled with the use of audio or videotape, the learning possibilities are greatly expanded and the opportunity is presented for highly constructive and imaginative thinking about self-improvement. Opportunity is there in abundance. We just do not avail ourselves of it. Yet it is easy to do so. It is also easy to make use of students to help you improve your teaching and your courses.

## Why use students' evaluation?

Johnson (1967) has really answered this question when he says: "It is often the individual student who knows best whether or not he is learning. It is the student who knows best when he cannot understand or already knows what is being discussed. It is the student who knows a course is stimulating him to learn more about a subject or whether it is boring him to death. It is a student who can best formulate these fundamental and personal questions so bothering him that he cannot proceed to other academic matters. It is the student who can best evaluate when he is beginning to integrate the process of learning with the problems he continually confronts in life." (p. 289-90).

Unless a teacher listens to what his students are saying he is depriving himself of valuable information about whether or not they are learning. Aristotle, in his Politics, pointed out that guests at a dinner party are in a better position to evaluate the merits of the meal than is the cook who prepared it. The same holds true for teaching. It is the consumers who have a better idea of whether they are actually learning than the instructor who teaches the course. Even if they are unable to assess accurately an instructor's mastery of his subject, they *are* able to say whether the subject was well organized, whether the material was communicated successfully, and whether the instructor displayed interest and enthusiasm in his presentation. Students, too, provide valuable feedback on their own reactions to a course of instruction, reactions at which an instructor can usually only guess. They can indicate whether their understanding was increased, their interest aroused and their curiosity stimulated. Evidence of such understanding, interest and curiosity is not necessarily proof of effective, long-time learning. However, it is unlikely that any meaningful, lasting learning will take place if such student reactions are lacking (Combs et al, 1974; Rogers, 1969).

If, as Austin & Lee (1966) have pointed out, one can accept the view that the ultimate measure of the teacher's effectiveness is his impact on the student, it seems inadvisable to neglect the sources most likely to yield information about this impact. Students are likely to be the best judges of a course of lectures by virtue of the fact that they are usually the only people who actually listen to them.

This is not to claim that student evaluation of their lecturers is unfailingly valid. It isn't. However, it really does not have to be, for, as Falk & Lee Dow (1971) suggest, it is only necessary to accept that a student's view reliably represents his reaction to the teaching he is or was receiving. It does not have to be accepted as a valid or true statement of what the teaching was actually like, only as a statement of how he, the student, experienced it. This is a unique contribution to evaluation for it cannot come from anywhere else. Whether the student's perspective is accurate or not is largely beside the point, for it is his attitude towards the instructor and the course which is vital. It is this attitude towards the instruction he is receiving which, to a large extent, determines how effectively he will learn (Mager, 1968). Students are constantly rating their teachers. The issue is really whether the instructor wants to find out what this rating is or whether he prefers to remain in ignorance about the way students perceive his course. If he chooses the first of these alternatives, he is in a position to use this information to improve both his course and his own performance.

This is one of the main purposes of using student evaluation to improve teaching. Some evidence does exist that this actually takes place, with teachers tending to change in the direction the students want as long as this accords with their course objectives (Terc, 1976). Where student feedback conflicts with a teacher's objectives, he is alerted to this problem and has the opportunity of dealing with it. It is rather pointless to insist, as some lecturers do, that if students do not see things the lecturer's way, it is the student's funeral. An approach more conducive to successful learning is to accept the validity of student perception and attempt to modify a course so that, while still retaining what the lecturer wants, it meets their needs more closely.

Empirical evidence does exist that many instructors are able to do this (e.g. Centra, 1972; Gage et al, 1963), using student ratings as a source of feedback on their teaching, and modifying their approach accordingly. Chisolm (1977) has, however, argued that despite the widespread use of student evaluation in the United States, no discernible improvements in teaching have resulted from it. The evidence is far from conclusive on this point. On theoretical grounds, however, one would expect an instructor who had information about his impact on students to improve his teaching and meet learning needs more effectively. Whether a lecturer actually would do so or not depends on the individual and the importance he attaches to his role as an instructor. As Shakespeare put it: "The fault, dear Brutus, lies not in our stars but in ourselves that we are underlings." Student evaluation would seem to provide a basis for lecturer self-improvement but one which he might prefer to ignore.

If information is sought from students at a number of points during the course, the value of such feedback is greatly enhanced. Four possibilities would be:

- At the beginning of a course. Information sought at this point would concern students' background and expectations.
- During the course. Rating scales could be used to provide feedback on *process*. A lecturer would gain some idea of how well his objectives were being achieved, how students were reacting to his teaching methods and the learning experiences he was providing. Such evaluation is "formative" in that it provides information on which the lecturer can act to "form" or "reform" his course while it is in progress.
- At the end of the course. Evaluation at this point is "summative" in that it looks at the *product* of the course. Again rating scales may be used in an evaluative way, these being employed together with assessment of student learning through examinations to provide information on how successful the attainment of course objectives has been.
- Some time after the conclusion of the course. Mager (1968) would see this as perhaps most important of all for, in his view,: "Learning is for the future; that is, the object of instruction is to facilitate some form of behaviour at a point after the instruction has been completed." Deriving information from students several years after they have completed the course assists the lecturer to answer the question: "Just how valuable is this course? Does it actually help students in later life?" I believe, as Mager does, that unless students do gain such benefit through exposure to a course, a lot of time and money has been spent for little purpose. We are incredibly wasteful of time, both ours and our students. Carl Sandburg said it so well: "Time is the coin of your life. It is the only coin you have, and only you can determine how it will be spent. Be careful lest you let other people spend it for you".

When we provide courses for students to attend, we should ensure we are giving them something of worth, and unless we collect systematic data on how they perceive what we present, we are unlikely ever to learn whether we are doing so. It may be unpalatable to face the fact that our students find our offerings useless, but, if this information helps us improve what we are doing, it is better than continuing to waste their time and ours year after year. This is, I feel, *the* rationale for the use of student evaluation. But it does not stand alone — there are other arguments advanced in its support.

## The pro and con of student evaluation

If the educational process is seen as essentially democratic, the use of student evaluation helps make the teaching-learning situation into a co-operative enterprise. This is particularly true if students are also involved in the identification of desirable learning outcomes, selection of appropriate content and structure, and design of a system of assessment capable of measuring which course objectives have been achieved. Even if student co-operation is not invoked to this extent, seeking their assistance through course evaluation instruments is likely to have a favourable motivational effect. Recognition is gratifying to all of us, and when we seek students' opinion we are recognizing their importance.

This opinion is likely to be of value in many ways. Not only do student rating scales provide information on teacher performance, but they can also be designed to furnish data on workloads, assessment procedures, course content, audio-visual media used in the course, and actual learning techniques which the student employed.

The case for student evaluation may seem impressive, yet many arguments have been mounted against its use in institutions of higher education (Stanton, 1974b). Although part of this resistance may stem from staff doubts about the competence of those who prepare such rating instruments, there remain serious objections to their use no matter who prepares them. These include claims: " . . . that student ratings are unreliable; that the ratings will favour an entertainer over the instructor who gets his material across effectively; that ratings are highly correlated with expected grades (a hard grader would thus get poor ratings) and that students are not competent judges of instruction since long-term benefits of a course may not be clear at the time it is rated." (Costin, et al., 1971, p.511).

Many objections revolve around the viewpoint that students are simply not capable of being objective evaluators. They don't really know what is good for them and, in fact, have no right to even try and evaluate their teacher who does know what is in their best interests. The seductive lecturer, for example, who puts on a good show, deceives them so completely that they are unable to detect differences in the content and importance of the information presented (Ware & Williams, 1975), just as they are incapable of distinguishing indoctrination from good teaching.

The research evidence we have does not support this type of objection. In his investigations of the faculty evaluation programme at the University of Washington, Guthrie (1954) could find no evidence for the claim that the rating of the popular, entertaining lecturer was inflated at the expense of his colleague who supposedly offered a more substantial course. Both Remmers (1963) and McKeachie (1969b) have supported Guthrie, concluding that students do know when they are learning, and that they use this as the basis of their rating rather than reacting to the personality of their lecturer. This evaluation, too, would seem to have stability over time, for Drucker & Remmers (1951) have showed that student ratings of instructors correlate well with ratings of the same instructor made by students ten years after graduation.

This finding would seem to offer little cheer to those who claim that students cannot really evaluate a teacher until they have left college or university and gained perspective on what was really valuable to them.

Another objection receiving little support from Guthrie was the unreliability claim. He found nothing to suggest that students' ratings were undependable and whimsical. On the contrary, he concluded that when as many as 25 student judgements were secured, the picture they gave of the course and of the instructor was quite stable. Further evidence from Lehmann (1961) indicated that ratings were not significantly affected by factors such as class size, sex of rater, or teacher's sex. Nor, in general, do the grades the students expect to receive correlate significantly with their ratings (Kent, 1967). However, on the few occasions where small correlations have been observed which link grades received and course rating, these seem to be due to greater interest in the course being shown by the students receiving better grades, rather than being the result of a reward effect.

In their review of the empirical studies in this area, Costin et al. (1971) concluded that: " . . . student ratings can provide reliable and valid information on the quality of courses and instruction . . . the criteria used by students in their rating of instructors had much more to do with the quality of the presentation of material than with the entertainment value of the course per se. Such attributes as preparedness, clarity, and stimulation of students' intellectual curiosity were typically mentioned by students in rating their best instructors." (p.530).

Their conclusion, that the lecturer who is highly rated by students is likely to be an outstanding teacher, has been confirmed by Hildebrand & Wilson (1970), and by McKeachie & Kulik (1975) who found students learnt most from those teachers rated as effective. However, it would be unwise to accept student rating as a complete evaluation of an instructor's teaching contribution. His work with higher degree students, his research contribution and his development of new courses are some of the other aspects which would need to be considered in an overall assessment.

Student evaluation is one source of information only, but it is one that has been overlooked in many countries other than the United States where it has been securely established for many years.

## Some ways of collecting information from students

As Roid (1971) has pointed out, course evaluation should properly be viewed as a total system involving five steps.
1. Stating values and expectancies related to courses.
2. Deciding upon methods for making observations on a course.
3. Collecting information using the methods chosen at the times it is necessary to make decisions.
4. Looking at the results to identify matches between expectations and estimates of what is or was actually happening in the course.
5. Investigating and using methods for adapting the course (if necessary) on the basis of results identified.

Something has been said earlier on most of these points and in this section I should like to concentrate primarily on the methods of gaining information from students.

Although interviews, both individual and group have been used, the amount of time involved has precluded the widespread employment of this method. Instead, deriving information from questionnaires and inventories handed out to students has proven to be the most popular choice. Economical of time and easy to administer, questionnaires, if well designed, can also provide much information. Possibly the most basic point is to include both closed and open questions. The following evaluation form, used at the University of Tasmania, begins with specific closed questions requiring the student to circle the appropriate response, and then provides for open responses on questions relating to course strengths, weaknesses and improvements.

## COURSE EVALUATION QUESTIONNAIRE
*Circle the alternative you feel is most appropriate*

### PART A

| | | | | |
|---|---|---|---|---|
| 1 How valuable an experience in itself was this course? | Of great value | Of considerable value | Of some value | Of little value |
| 2 Has this course been academically relevant to your programme of study? | Of great relevance | Of considerable relevance | Of some relevance | Of little relevance |
| 3 Has this course been intellectually stimulating? | Great intellectual stimulation | Considerable intellectual stimulation | Some intellectual stimulation | Little intellectual stimulation |
| 4 How efficiently has this course been run? | With great efficiency | With considerable efficiency | With some efficiency | With little efficiency |
| 5 How confidently can you now (as a result of this course) identify significant points or central issues in this area? | With great confidence | With considerable confidence | With some confidence | With little confidence |
| 6 How successfully was the work-load required in this course adjusted to the credit points offered? | With great success | With considerable success | With some success | With little success |

7 Which of the following circumstances lie primarily behind your being in the course?
   (1) professional/career interest:
   (2) personal interest in the subject matter:
   (3) the staff conducting the course:
   (4) to make up credit points:
   (5) to satisfy prerequisites or corequisites:
   (6) strong academic advice:
   (7) advice from other students:
   (8) other reasons (specify):

## PART B

8 What were the best features of the course?

9 What were the worst features of the course?

10 What changes would you recommend in the course?

11 Any other comments.

This approach has some similarities to that used at the University of Washington (Langen, 1966; Slobin & Nicholls, 1969). The advantage of employing the *actual* University of Washington "Survey of Student Opinion of Teaching" is the long period of time it has been in service and the evidence of reliability and validity which has accumulated. The same may be said for the Purdue Rating Scale (Remmers & Weisbrodt, 1965) which has been in use since 1930.

The virtue of questionnaires such as these is their relative brevity. Long evaluation forms, particularly if used at several points during a course, soon become boring to the students who are responding to them. As well as keeping forms short, there are certain other principles which, if observed, are likely to result in more usable information. One of these is to administer the scale during a normal class period and have it returned as students leave the room. This ensures a 100 per cent return, something sadly lacking when students take them away to be completed and later returned. If the presence of the lecturer in the room is seen as likely to prejudice the response accuracy, outside assistance may be sought. Staff Development Centres as described in the next chapter can provide such a service. An additional safeguard lies in anonymity, with students' names not appearing on the evaluation form. To further enhance such anonymity, it is preferable that students drop their completed forms into a box as they depart from the room, rather than hand them in to their lecturer.

For the actual writing of items, Davis et al. (1974) suggest the following guidelines. Firstly, ask questions about how the instruction affected student development such as "Was the lecture material organized so that you could take notes easily?", rather than questions about student achievement itself. Secondly, only include questions students would be able to answer from their own experience. A query: "Were you able to see the relationships between the various topics of the course?" would meet this criteria. Thirdly, ask questions in such a way that the answers will enable you to take some action. For example; "Did you have the opportunity to participate in class discussions?" A list of topics for possible inclusion in a student opinion questionnaire with illustrative questions has also been provided by Davis et al.

A  Instructor Involvement
1  The instructor was enthusiastic when presenting course material.
2  The instructor seemed interested in teaching.
3  The instructor used examples or personal experiences which helped to get points across in class.
4  The instructor seemed to be concerned with whether the students learned the material.
5  The instructor was friendly and relaxed in front of the class.

B  Student Interest.
1  I felt this course challenged me intellectually.
2  I was generally attentive in class.
3  I intend to take more courses in this subject.

C   Student-Instructor Interaction
    1   The instructor encouraged students to express opinions.
    2   I had ample opportunity to ask questions.
    3   The instructor appeared receptive to new ideas.

D   Course Demands
    1   The instructor attempted to cover too much material.
    2   The instructor lectured above my level of comprehension.

E   Course Organization
    1   I could see how the concepts in this course were interrelated.
    2   The class lectures made for easy note-taking.
    3   I knew where the course was heading most of the time.

F   Grading and Examinations
    1   The grading system was adequately explained.
    2   The answers to exam questions were adequately explained after the exam
        was given.
    3   Course objectives were reflected in the exams.

G   Relevance of the Course.
    1   I could see how the course material could be applied to my personal
        problems.
    2   I could see how the course material is pertinent to my major field of interest.
    3   The instructor made me aware of current problems in the field.

The basic scales considered so far have been standardized. However, an evaluative questionnaire designed by the lecturer along the lines suggested by Davis et al., will, of necessity, become more of a personal document. This may be desirable, for, despite the previously mentioned advantages of using a standardized instrument, such a practice suffers from two serious weaknesses. The first of these is the likelihood of collecting information on rating forms unsuitable to the particular course in question. The items on traditional scales may be too generalized to help the individual teacher. Secondly, the results produced by such evaluative instruments may be difficult to interpret unless teachers can compare their results with others. This they are often loath to do. Because of students' tendency to rate their teachers leniently (e.g. Flood-Page, 1974) it may be difficult for instructors to locate their strengths and weaknesses. To overcome this problem, both Purdue University and the University of Michigan have adopted a "Cafeteria" system which features a core of five items used by all staff and a catalogue of about 200 items from which an instructor could construct a 40-item rating form. After the instructor has selected his item, his rating forms are computer printed. Student responses are also handled by the computer which provides printouts on an instructor's absolute and relative standing on each item. Thus interpretability is improved and instructors receive feedback about the specific things in which they are concerned. The "Cafeteria" system does seem a great improvement over traditional rating scales, though without the services of a computer its value would be reduced.
An interesting way of deriving additional benefit from rating scales, whether of the "Cafeteria" type or not, is for the lecturer to fill out the same form as that issued to his students. In so doing he should try to see himself through the eyes of his students. A comparison of responses enables the instructor to see if his students perceive his

teaching performance in the same way as he does. If what a teacher thinks he is doing coincides reasonably well with what his students see him as doing, his perception is realistic. However, if there is considerable discrepancy between the two evaluations, the teacher is unlikely to be facilitating learning particularly well. As a result of insensitivity to his students he is likely to encounter misinterpretation and misunderstanding (Stanton, 1971). His assumptions about what is happening in his class are out of touch with the reality as experienced by his students.

A rather different approach to this issue of reality — of finding what is really happening in a course — is to administer the same evaluation form twice (Stanton, 1970). The first administration is before the course begins, its intention being to tap student expectancy. The second is given at the end of the course to provide a measure of the reality, how students felt once the course was completed. The intention here is to discover to what extent interest in the course has increased or decreased as a result of students' exposure to it. Mager (1968) would suggest that a if a lecturer is unable to maintain or increase the degree of interest shown by students on entry to his course, he is doing more harm than good. If, through his handling of a course, he decreases student interest in his subject, he is reducing the likelihood of further approach behaviour and future use of the course content. Things disliked have a way of being avoided so it is as well for us to know whether we are actively inoculating our students against any further interest in our subject.

Perhaps all this talk of multiple administrations of rating scales sounds like a lot of work. It isn't really, and the results far outweigh the effort involved. Still, there is an alternative method. Silberman and Allender (1974) suggest evaluation through a "course description." Students are asked to write a 15 minute description of the course for the benefit of a hypothetical student who is considering enrolling in a subsequent semester. They are left completely free to decide how they will write their description. From their writings, two measures are derived. The first is evaluative tone, defined as the value students place on the course. This is quantified by adding up the number of positive and negative statements made, including comments about the course's value, enjoyment or difficulty. Impact is the second measure, operationalized as the extent to which the course has contributed to the student's personal change. Again, a pre-and post-course description would prove enlightening in terms of the expectancy and the reality.

Though student evaluation of course and instructor is primarily concerned with the learning *process* it may, as has been described at several points in this chapter, provide information on the *product* of learning. However, more traditional forms of student assessment remain as the prime source of data on this issue and these we now consider.

### Why do we examine students?

The term "examination" may be defined very narrowly or very broadly. In the context of the present discussion it seems appropriate to take the latter path, interpreting "examinations" to cover all forms of assessment applied in higher education courses and not restricting the term to formal three-hour papers given at the end of the academic year. If examinations are looked at in this way, there are several main purposes for which they are used.

The first of these is student assessment, with performance in examinations providing information about the knowledge, skills and attitudes presumably acquired as a result of the course they have undertaken.

Assignment of a grade, such as distinction, credit, pass or fail is a second purpose. This is a summative judgement based on the educational product of what students have accomplished. A third purpose of examinations involves evaluation of the effectiveness of instruction through letting the lecturer know how effective he has been. Use as an instructional device to assist student learning is the fourth main purpose. In these last two cases the examination acts in a formative way, assisting instructor and students to improve their performance through feedback about areas of weakness. A fifth reason for using examinations invokes the concept of motivation, with students being spurred to more diligent study efforts through the knowledge that they will be tested.

Not all of these purposes are relevant to the present context which looks at ways in which the instructor may derive feedback on the effectiveness of his teaching. How useful examinations are in providing this information is open to question. As Rowntree (1974) has commented:

"Most educational testing concentrates on what the student can do, and usually on what he can do immediately after the course and under threat of assessment, rather than on what he can or will do some time after the course is over and of his own volition. (thus examinations take place right after a course not simply for administrative convenience, but because of the fact that most of what students learn, . . . may be so irrelevant to their interests that the learning will have evaporated through lack of practice if the evaluation is delayed by more than a week or two.)" (P. 65. Author's brackets).

Although his remark was made in the secondary school context, it seems capable of generalization to higher education. If what we measure is short term memory for material held in storage until the examination is over, we have little real basis for using such results as indication that learning has taken place. Yet, attempting to assess long-term learning well after the completion of a course presents considerable administrative difficulties. Even if we can accept that examinations given immediately a course ends provide valid evidence of student learning, the amount of "feedback" to both lecturer and student is likely to be minimal. Although lip service is paid to the concept that one of the chief purposes of examinations is to provide information leading to improved learning, in actuality this is not widely practised.

In theory, much assessment is intended to be diagnostic in nature, particularly that administered during the course. As the student receives back his test or assignment he can, supposedly, see where he has gone wrong, and receive guidance on how he might rectify his errors. Often, no attempt is made by lecturers to use assessment to serve this diagnostic function. Even when it does occur, if the feedback is delayed through slow marking, its impact is greatly diluted. How rarely, too, does the lecturer actually use the results of such assessment to learn about his own performance. It can provide information to help him see how *he* is doing as well as providing information on the progress of his students. Such formative functions of examinations are swamped in too many cases by the summative aspects of grading processes. Each piece of work submitted must be marked and graded, this being seen as the lecturer's main function. This behaviour is reflected in the prevalence of work handed back to students with no comment other than a single letter grade or mark. Not all tertiary teachers do this, but it is a practice that is far too common.

One possible way of improving matters is to shift some of the emphasis away from assessing students towards evaluating the effectiveness of teaching through the use of testing for mastery. Such an approach differs markedly from the traditional concept of grading students on the normal curve so that a certain percentage must always fall into the various grading categories. This norm — referenced testing compares students with each other so that a few do very badly, a few do very well, and the majority do moderately well. The concept of mastery means the pre-determination of performance levels which students either attain or do not attain. Thus criterion-referenced tests establish if a student has reached the criterion set, this being expressed in terms of course objectives. Once we move to a mastery approach, examination results do become very helpful in providing feedback on teaching effectiveness. If students are unsuccessful in reaching the course criterion, this says something about the teaching provided. Whereas, under a norm-referenced system, the number of students falling into the distinction, credit, pass and fail categories may be manipulated according to the normal curve proportions, such adjustment does not occur with criterion-referenced testing. A student may pass, get credits, or fail depending to a considerable extent on how well or how poorly the instructor has helped him learn.

Wide adoption of such an approach will, however, require considerable attitude change in institutions of higher education. Imagine the consternation if every student passed in a particular course. Remarks like: "Too easy. Prostitution of academic standards. No rigour" would fall like rain upon the head of the unfortunate instructor. Not many people would be brave enough to suggest that the results were due to good teaching. Few would point out that here was a teacher who had been very successful in setting up precise objectives, providing a set of experiences which facilitated student learning, and assessing students on their attainment of the objectives. To colleagues conditioned to the normal curve, this explanation would be unacceptable. Such results could not be the result of good teaching, only of lowering standards. Rowntree's (1974) example of the secondary school examiner who, when it was suggested that programmes would soon enable all students to pass O-level mathematics, said: "Oh no, they won't, we'll just raise the standard," reflects this attitude in another way.

A mastery approach to testing is likely to promote improved student learning by stimulating instructors to clarify their objectives and motivating students towards achieving certain essential goals. If the examinations to be used are prepared before the course begins and if students are informed early about the kinds of achievement it will require of them, then the examinations will have a significant effect in directing the activities of both students and instructor (Ebel, 1958). Learning will be further enhanced if questions are discussed soon after the examination has been completed. We miss many opportunities to use examinations as learning experiences for both students and ourselves by not engaging in such discussion.

Although the movement towards mastery testing is growing in strength, it is, as yet, not widely used in institutions of higher education. Still firmly entrenched is the traditional pattern of comparing students on the basis of examination performance, and marking them in terms of their responses to questions about the course content. The vehicle most commonly used is the essay, followed by objective tests, short answer questions, structured questions, open-book tests, practical work, student self-assessment and orals, not necessarily in order of importance.

Essays and objective tests dominate the testing field. The other alternatives are of relatively minor importance, and this is unfortunate, for the value of their particular contribution has been too frequently overlooked. Open-book examinations, for example in which students are permitted to take books in to the examination room and look up material, seems to be very applicable in a professional education context

(Beard, 1970). A basic skill in such areas is the ability to find facts and figures quickly, to know where to look and how to go about extracting relevant information.

Student self-assessment is another greatly under-used technique, though for more obvious reasons. Risk is involved, for the tertiary institution is seen as placing society's stamp of approval on those it graduates. If it graduated students found to be inferior and inadequate, its reputation would suffer, and rightly so. The chance of this happening as a result of students' evaluating themselves has not been adequately investigated but my own studies suggest that it is a function of maturity. (Stanton, 1978a). Older students seem to be more realistic in their self-assessment though they are often too hard on themselves. Undergraduates, particularly in first and second years, tend to overvalue their own efforts, possibly through lack of experience in what constitutes adequate academic work. This would suggest students should be given some experience in self-assessment, perhaps in non-critical areas, from the time of entry into higher education. Such experience carries with it considerable educational value in students coming to terms with the criteria upon which academic standards are based. It is also an important learning experience for lecturers who are forced to justify their own assessment procedures.

Over-reliance on one or two examining techniques runs counter to the concept that students differ and should be given the opportunity to learn and be tested in a variety of ways. The view is reflected in the increasing popularity of continuous assessment which takes into account all aspects of a student's work during his course. Thus, tutorial essays, practicals, seminar contributions and dissertations as well as written examinations should be considered, since all provide feedback to teachers and students. Continuous assessment is seen as reducing nervous tension because all is not lost or gained on one examination though it has also been remarked that such an approach ensures: " . . . that students now have ulcers as well as nervous breakdowns." (Rowntree, 1974. p. 134). Within the written examination itself, it seems desirable to have a diversity of methods to cater for individual differences. However, admirable as this concept may be, in practice our examinations still predominantly favour the essay and objective type question, which exposes them to serious criticism.

## The examination system — weaknesses and improvements

Cox (1967a) sums up much of the critical feeling about essay examinations when he writes:

"One of the difficulties here is that there is often no clear statement of what the college is trying to do. Even in vocational subjects like medicine, there is still serious disagreement as to what makes a good doctor. If it is not clear what the examinations are trying to do, it is difficult to assess whether they are doing it well or badly. If a change is made in an examining system, the lack of any agreed criteria prevents the fact finding which would show whether the change was worthwhile or not." (p.353).

He continues to point out that changing the examination system is difficult, not only because assessment is made awkward by the general lack of agreement on educational aims, but also because, once it is set up, it gains a momentum of its own. It then becomes easier to maintain this momentum rather than to change it in response to information, the worth of which is difficult to evaluate.

That some change is necessary seems apparent from Cox's (1967b) review of the use of examinations in higher education. He is especially critical of their unreliability, quoting evidence of different examiners giving widely different marks to the same script and of the same examiner giving the same script widely different marks on two different occasions. Sometimes, this variability is so great that a random allocation of marks would have been nearly as useful (Bull, 1956). In the face of evidence such as this, which has been available for several decades, the remarkable thing is the calm assurance with which tertiary teachers believe in their ability to ". . . carry around in their heads an unfailing correct conception of an absolute standard." (Dale, 1959). This assumption survives all evidence to the contrary, that, in fact, examination marks gained by a particular student may be more a function of the examiner than of the examinee (Pieron, 1963).

The content validity of examinations may also be questioned on the grounds of their ability to sample only a small fraction of the work covered in course. A wider criticism involves face validity, that students see little relationship between what they do in the examination situation and what they have been doing during the year. This doubt on validity has been sharply pointed up by Hoyt (1965) in his demonstration that college grades showed little or no relationship to any measures of adult accomplishment.

Attempts to improve the embattled system have had relatively little large-scale success. Increasing the number of essay markers and divising more rigorous marking techniques have not produced the anticipated improvement in reliability though shortening essays and providing a structure with sub-headings has been more successful (Cox, 1967b). However, using this latter method, reliability is gained at the expense of the opportunity for synthesis afforded by the essay format.

Use of objective tests has been oft seen as the answer to the weaknesses of the essay type examination and their use has increased dramatically particularly in the United States. Advantages claimed for this type of testing include a broad covering of the field of knowledge, reduced emphasis on speed and verbal fluency, provision of more diagnostic information on a student's abilities, quick knowledge of results, and reduction in marking time. This latter advantage would be balanced by the greatly increased time required to design the items. Criticism of objective testing abounds, too, the main one being the emphasis on rote learning of course content and convergent thinking which is encouraged. Objective-type questions are limiting in other ways for they preclude the development of reasoned arguments and allow the student no opportunity to show his ability in the organization of course material.

As the weaknesses of this type of question are not those of the essay, it would appear reasonably to effect a blending. As no single examination is completely satisfactory in terms of both reliability and validity (Ager & Weltman, 1967), a variety of techniques might be used to examine different course aims. Objective items are well suited to a wide sampling of content, whereas essay questions are very useful for assessing students' ability to manipulate material through use of analysis, synthesis and evaluation. Gronlund (1968) is very helpful in suggesting various ways in which achievement tests might be organized while McKeachie (1969a) provides valuable ideas on test preparation in general. Another source of ideas is the students themselves. On many occasions I have set students the assignment of constructing their own examination paper. This is excellent revision and keeps me well supplied with examination questions, often better ones than I would have developed myself.

Generation of suitable examination questions is, however, unlikely to effect much improvement in the system. The basic issue, referred to again and again in the literature, is that of the instructor's aims. Once he knows what he wants his course to achieve, he can select the most appropriate means of assessing his students. That is, his assessment method is virtually determined by his objectives and herein lies the path to improvement of the examination system — clarification of aims. As Himmelweit (1967) says:

"Lecturers must accept that they won't find an adequate examination system until they are willing to state clearly the objectives of the training, the type of knowledge, outlook and behaviour they would expect from a student who has done well in the course and one who has done badly."

# Chapter 10

# Can higher education be improved?

## *Is teaching in need of improvement?*

The title of this chapter assumes that improvement in teaching is necessary. Many of the comments I have made earlier indicate my acceptance of this assumption, at least in general terms. However, it is undeniably the case that much excellent teaching does take place in many tertiary institutions which succeed in educating large numbers of students to adequate standards of professional competence, equipping them with the requisite knowledge and skills for success in their chosen fields. This achievement is often overlooked by critics. However, given this very positive accomplishment, I think most tertiary level teachers would admit that there is considerable room for improvement. Just as good teaching exists, so does much very poor teaching which leads to comments such as that made by O'Dowd (1967):

" . . . I am disturbed and annoyed at the dilatoriness and timidity of higher education. How can a major social institution care so little about understanding its central function. It is evident that research into teaching is nonexistent in most universities and is only an incidental activity in others. The infinitesimal percentage of the higher education budget devoted to research into educational results and the improvement of teaching is shameful . . . Higher education, by its very resistance or inattention to the study of its major activity, has denied itself the very means by which it can improve . . . innovation, invention and imagination in the teaching process are discouraged by the very privacy of the teaching situation." (p 249).

O'Dowd's emphasis on lack of interest in improving teaching echoes a basic theme of this book. Change, as it occurs in higher education, is not rapid. This seems particularly true of teaching processes which seem little different from those used many decades ago. The reason may be that we have discovered already those things which work best in educating students and so further investigation is fruitless. Few would ostensibly espouse this view, because it runs counter to all tenets preached by institutions of higher education where rational man dispassionately inquiring into truth is the accepted model. Yet the behaviour of many academics in refusing to study the teaching process as a worthy field of endeavour implies its acceptance. Educational research may not have been an outstanding success in the past, though, as earlier chapters have indicated, it has made significant contributions to our ideas about how university and college teaching might be improved. Before these are further considered, it might be well to inquire why such strong resistance to change is apparent in higher education.

## *Obstacles to change*

Some of the more important of these have been outlined by Adelson (1974). First, the incentive structure of tertiary institutions pushes faculty in conventional directions such as designing research rather than designing improvements in teaching. The reward system operates to ensure the maintenance of such behaviour for it is seen as the path to advancement. An individual academic operates within a framework of institutional attitudes and values, and teaching will tend to have low priority for him if it is seen as having little status within the institution. Unless an institution's reward system is altered in such a way that promotion is significantly related " . . . to involvement in innovation or development of teaching and learning" (Harding & Sayer, 1975) there is little likelihood of significant improvement in tertiary teaching.

Second, the finances of institutions are a constraint on what can be accomplished. Normally, teaching receives a relatively low priority with few resources specifically directed towards innovation (Eraut, 1975). Money is available for maintenance of existing teaching patterns. It is often lacking to fund changes in those patterns.

The self-perpetuating character of the educational system is seen by Adelson as a third obstacle to innovation. Students are produced in the image of their instructors, and therefore, ultimately, instructors in the image of their predecessors. Such a pattern is unlikely to generate much dissatisfaction with the existing state of affairs, so little desire for change becomes apparent. Educational innovators, attempting to reform a system they see as inadequate, often ignore this strong sense of stability, of leaving things as they are "because they worked all right for me". Any innovation in education, by definition, requires some people to change their ways, yet innovators have a penchant for expecting other people to change, not themselves. People don't really like to change, for, to admit it is necessary implies they are inadequate in their present functioning. None of us really enjoys admitting to incompetency so our resistance to change is not surprising. As educational systems are made up of people, they tend to remain static.

A further obstacle is also a matter of human personality. Just as we tend to resist change as disruptive to our existing behaviour, we fear the risks involved if we are tempted to innovate. These fears are many, including loss of status, failure, and unfavourable reactions from colleagues. Rather than run such risks, we may choose to do nothing, ignoring Emerson's advice to "do the thing you fear and the death of fear is certain." As long as we never attempt to change our teaching methods we will never learn if our fears, which are often more illusionary than real, are groundless.

After adding several other equally impressive reasons to his list, Adelson comes to the one he regards as most potent, the tertiary teacher's lack of experience in, and knowledge about, implementing change. They have, he says:

" . . . lots of experience at generating the knowledge which others use to change things; they have lots of experience convincing others to change things; they have lots of experience describing changes that ought to be made and decrying the lack of change where they believe it to be needed. But . . . they do not have much nitty-gritty experience at actually perpetuating change." (p 233).

This lack of experience about implementing change is easily understandable in the light of the point made earlier. Advocating change for other people and other institutions is a relatively safe pastime; suggesting self-change is a far riskier and more threatening procedure.

Despite the rather formidable array of reasons explaining why change is unlikely to occur, some innovations in higher education do exist. Many of these, such as peer teaching and individualized instruction have been discussed in earlier chapters, while institutions like the Open University in England and the University Without Walls in the United States represent successful large-scale innovation. Despite such examples, Oettinger (1969), among others, would question the value of innovation in education on grounds that it is only the appearance of such innovation which takes place. He is referring here to pilot schemes which operate under "hot-house" conditions and are rarely generalizable to a more normal environment. When the attempt is made, the "promising" innovations collapse in failure because conditions in such an environment are far from "hot-house" and the numbers of students involved are much greater. To support his claim, Oettinger quotes the example of language laboratories which are now underused or completely neglected in many institutions. Intention and reality rarely coincide, he contends, pointing to the lack of correspondence between the theory which leads to the adoption of an innovation and the practice that ensues. Though there is some truth in such a viewpoint, Oettinger's criticism does scant justice to many innovations. Methods of individualized instruction such as the Keller plan, for example, have proven to be readily transferable to many different educational environments. Successful innovation within universities and colleges *is* possible, and we now consider ways in which it might be achieved.

## Changing the Teaching Practices of Higher Education

Although a number of possible strategies have been suggested, relatively few hold out great promise of success. Self-analysis, often mooted as the best way for teachers to improve their performance, is suspect due to our relative inability to view ourselves realistically (Centra, 1972). Use of a team of outside experts to remodel an institution's teaching procedures has proven effective (Sanford, 1971), but would seem to be precluded on the grounds both of high cost and unavailability of sufficiently expert teams. A less costly alternative would be to develop a system of classroom observation by colleagues — a method outlined earlier. Though little experimental evidence is available on the effectiveness of this approach in encouraging innovatory teaching practices, it would seem to have considerable potential. Audio-video feedback, too, would appear to be a valuable aid in increasing teachers' self-awareness. However, to be effective, such feedback needs to be focused (Centra, 1972). That is, the videotape or audiotape is stopped at selected places and the viewers' attention directed to specific cues or behaviour. Where a lecturer simply views a replay without interruption or guidance, he is unlikely to modify his instructional behaviour (Rezler & Anderson, 1971). This guidance function is one which might be undertaken by an Instructional Development Centre. Such a Centre, too, would be useful in administering and processing student evaluation forms, suggested earlier as one of the more effective means of encouraging change in teaching practices.

## Instructional Development Centres

Though these Centres may be established according to different models (Hall, 1977b) and may go under rather different names, such as Educational Research Units, Centres for Advancement of Teaching & Learning, Learning & Development Centres, they share a basic purpose of assisting in the improvement of higher education and the creation of better learning conditions within the institutions in which they are established. Basically they attempt to achieve this aim in a number of ways. One of these is through *service activities,* which include consulting with individuals or groups of staff members, conducting seminars and workshops on learning and instructional procedures, and assisting staff to conduct instructional development projects. Another is undertaking *research* directed towards increasing basic knowledge about the teaching-learning process and developing more effective instructional programmes. A third approach is through *teaching* — the provision of courses directed towards staff development. Two activities mentioned earlier, provision of guidance in the use of audio and videotape feedback and the administration of student questionnaires fall within the Centre's service function and their work in this area is well illustrated by the Clinic to Improve University Teaching (CIUT) at the University of Massachusetts where a very comprehensive model has been developed (Sheehan, 1976). The procedure followed is:

- A member of CIUT interviews a lecturer to clarify why he wants help.
- Data on the lecturer's teaching skill is collected by means of student questionnaires, videotapes, classroom observations, audiotapes, interviews with students, lecturer self-ratings, copies of course objectives, assignments, and examinations.
- From this data, teaching strengths and weaknesses are located.
- The CIUT member makes a detailed diagnosis of the weaknesses, aided by further sharply focused questionnaire data from students as to probable causes and remedies.
- Implementation of instructional improvement procedures based on this diagnosis follows.
- Students again provide information through questionnaires as an evaluation of the changed instructional strategies, and further modification takes place.
- Final evaluation of the lecturer's teaching skill.

Theoretically, this model should lead to improved teaching, yet the amount of time involved is great, even with the use of computers to process the questionnaires. My chief concern is with the demands placed on students. It is one thing to seek their help in improving courses, but where so many evaluative instruments are involved, I think their goodwill might soon be eroded. Yet such a detailed procedure may be necessary if any really important changes are to be made in instructional procedures. Most of the things we now do to achieve this end seem quite ineffective, so CIUT's approach may be an indication of the way in which improvement agencies must work if they are to have any effect at all.

Other methods of faculty development do exist. Informal discussion groups between new appointees and more experienced staff members on topics such as problems involved in tertiary teaching, objectives, and assessment procedures, prove quite helpful, but their value in achieving improved instruction has not been convincingly demonstrated. Also, even when such activities are promoted by Instructional Development Centres, attendance is not large.

It has been suggested that such groups work better within their own faculties rather than on an institution-wide basis and Abercrombie (1968) has described such a pattern. She outlines the work done by a small unit set up within the school of architecture at the University College, London. The basic functions of service, research and teaching still apply in these more specialized centres, but because their activities are more closely integrated with the particular school faculty or department involved, the potentiality for effecting change would seem to be enhanced. Something akin to an educational community may be created in which innovation is made less threatening and easier to accomplish.

Encouraging tertiary staff to change their teaching procedures, whether the effort be directed towards individual faculties or the institution as a whole, really involves a three-phased programme (De Bloois & Adler, 1973). Initially *awareness activities* are provided. These might include provision of a newsletter series offering information about educational innovation, mini-reports of successful innovations actually taking place on campus, announcements about coming seminars and opportunities to apply for teaching development grants, and request forms through which an individual may request assistance. In addition to circulating a newsletter, an Instructional Improvement Centre might raise staff awareness by conducting seminars on topics such as lecturing, individualization of instruction, assessment procedures and use of media. A second phase involves *faculty support activities,* where staff attempting to improve their courses, have individual consultations with Centre members and are provided with small grants to help them develop new learning materials. *Instructional Development activities* comprise the third phases of the programme. Large grants could be awarded to subsidize released time, perhaps a term or semester, in which a staff member would work with Centre personnel to produce new learning materials and develop new course structures.

This three-phase programme has much to recommend it as a means of effecting instructional change, but rarely has it actually been implemented so systematically. What usually happens is that some of the activities mentioned are put into practice on a piecemeal basis. Many Instructional Development Centres, being starved of funds, are unable to support staff innovations with grants, large or small. The assistance they do provide is more in terms of a consultative service in which their expertise is placed at the disposal of the particular teacher wishing to modify his instructional procedures. Where a number of instructors are concerned about a problem, seminars or workshops are provided. Sometimes these may form a systematic sequence, but more frequently they are complete in themselves, designed to meet a specific need such as assistance to staff in acquiring a particular skill. Production of a slide-tape programme, for example, or techniques involved in conducting small groups are both popular topics, as is a micro-teaching type clinic on lecturing skills, where videotape feedback on performance is an integral feature.

Such in-service programmes can take many forms. One interesting procedure was followed at the University of Utah (Kapfer & Della-Piana, 1974) where a two-phased programme operated. Although it was designed for teaching fellows, the approach has wide applicability and is at present being used at the University of Tasmania in a modified form. Initially staff were invited to attend a workshop designated as a "stepping-off point" for participants rather than as a self-contained activity. The programme consisted of three one-hour introductory sessions on teaching proficiency assessment, personalized instruction and test construction. Sessions embraced multi-media presentations, speakers addressing large groups, informal discussion, and opportunities for questions-and-answers. Packets of materials on each of the three topics were distributed and discussed. Phase two was a follow up to this workshop in which participants selected one of the three topics to work on during the year. This they pursued with assistance from Centre staff as required, often producing material which led to a considerable change in the way they conducted their courses.

Instructional Development Centres can make available the various forms of assistance and expertise described above. Many of them, too, provide comprehensive audio-visual media services, not only making such material available but also helping teaching staff to use it effectively by intergrating it into their courses. Despite this wide range of activities in which Centres engage, however, doubts about their effectiveness in making any significant impact on higher education remains. Such doubt resides not only in the breasts of those outside the Centres, but also bedevils many of us who staff them. Perhaps conflicting ideas about role is the basis of this doubt. While we do reach out to faculty with our newsletters, seminars and workshops, our predominate mode of operation is to let them come to us when they require help. This is a very low key approach, perhaps engendered by the oft-repeated warning to Centre personnel to be careful about offending academics in the institutions in which they operate, to keep a low profile and by so doing reduce the threat of their existence. For, by their very presence on campus, Centres are a threat, an implied criticism of staff who should be teaching better than they are.

This is particularly true if they are cast in an evaluative role, for at least in English and Australian universities and colleges, academic staff greet with horror the idea that their teaching performance should be monitored in any way. Canadian and American institutions do not, as a rule, share this feeling, for systematic observation of teaching abilities in the consideration of promotion to higher academic rank has been used quite extensively in those countries. Part of the conflict for Instructional Development Centres, then, is doubt about whether they should play a passive, non-threatening role, helping those who seek them out, or become more aggressive, actively seeking to "sell" educational advice, and perhaps playing a part in evaluating teachers for promotion. However, if Centre staff are seen as "inspectors" evaluating staff teaching, they are unlikely to be approached for advice, for such action could be interpreted as a confession of weakness. Yet, as has been pointed out (e.g. McMillan, 1975), the faculty who do seek advice and participate in seminars and workshops are those likely to need help the least. The less motivated faculty are the ones who probably need to alter their instructional most, yet they are left unaffected by the passive approach of Centre personnel.

Furedy (1975) has claimed that Instructional Development Centres aim at an image of a well-ordered resource centre staffed by competent and concerned scholars acting as catalysts in the university or college system. The idea is that the individuals and departments who receive useful services will return to their departments as "seeders" of the Centres ideas and practices. However, as she points out, it seems that higher education institutions, at least in the United Kingdom and Australia, have relegated to the Instructional Development Centres the task of improving teaching while leaving untouched a system of academic rank which makes no provision for the evaluation of a lecturer's teaching abilities. It is this basic conflict between Centres devoted to the improvement of teaching and a system which appears to leave good teaching unrewarded which has lead to charges of "tokenism." Is the establishment of these Centres little more than a public relations exercise, demonstrating that a particular institution is really concerned with its teaching performance and has done something about it?

Teaching staff really hold the key to whether Centres can be more than a token. In reality, it seems that an Instructional Development Centre can be viable only in terms of academic staff being willing to admit they can be helped. Most students who enter a normal academic course are usually conscious of a need to learn. However, academic staff, who may be aware of the need to continue learning within their own discipline, often do not accept the fact they have something to learn about their own classroom performance. Unless instructors can accept this, there is little future for a Centre of the sort described. Experience in the United States, Canada, the United Kingdom and Australia suggests that staff development courses have little drawing power unless some reward is provided for improved teaching performance (Flood-Page, 1975). Another reason may be their episodic nature and lack of continuity. Would more systematic training for tertiary teachers provide the answer?

Critics of higher education point out that, unlike their primary and secondary school brethren, teachers in higher education receive no formal preservice training. Their possession of certain academic qualifications, and some evidence of research interest, is usually sufficient to ensure appointment, their ability to teach effectively being assumed. It is also assumed that a tertiary teacher has no need of the background in educational theory thought to be necessary for school teachers. Instructional Development Centres normally attempt to meet this lack of preparation in the staff they advise by a rather piecemeal approach, but there is a growing awareness that a more comprehensive course, something along the lines of a Diploma of Education, might help to improve the quality of higher education (Miller, 1976). It does not necessarily follow that such a training will lead to improvement, for, as Popham (1971) has demonstrated, the preparation that secondary school teachers receive does not appear to make a measurable difference in student learning. In fact, Popham raises the fundamental question of whether teachers have any special expertise at all. His experiments, replicated by Moody & Bausell (1973) with the same results, suggest that students taught by experienced, certified teachers learn no better than students taught by individuals who have had no training or experience as teachers. These finding have been questioned in terms of the achievement tests used (Good, et al, 1975) but Popham's work should caution us against too-ready acceptance of the view that teacher education courses are the answer to the ills of higher education.

Teacher education should, however, make a difference. As an article of faith, all educators normally subscribe to such a view and intuitively it seems unassailable. Unfortunately, as far as higher education is concerned, we have no real evidence to support or disprove this view. So few diploma type courses are in existence that some time will have to elapse before the effect on graduates is felt. The topics most likely to be found in Tertiary Teaching Courses are the following (Miller, 1976).

1. The Tertiary Student    a. Needs and Interests
    b. Adult Learning
    c. Problems and Counselling

2. Tertiary Level Courses    a. Aims and Objectives
    b. Design
    c. Self-Instructional Techniques

3 Lecturing    a. Function
    b. Preparation and Techniques
    c. Use of Educational Media

4. Small Group Teaching    a. Types and Purposes
    b. Leadership
    c. Discussion Techniques

5. Evaluation    a. Student Learning
    b. Teacher Effectiveness
    c. Course Design

It is difficult to take issue with such a course. If a substantial number of lecturers were exposed to this education, spread over a two-year period while they were actively teaching, an improvement in the general level of tertiary instruction should follow. I would stress the in-service rather than the pre-service nature of this training. Pre-service courses run the risk of raising problems in which students are uninterested and of providing answers which fall on deaf ears as a result of this. With in-service courses, instructors, because of their on-going practical experience, are more likely to feel some need to find answers to the problems they are already encountering. Perhaps such courses conducted by Instructional Development Centres, in co-operation with other interested educationalists from their own institution, may be the best means we have for promoting innovation in higher education, particularly if it can be coupled to an apprentice-type system for new teachers in which more experienced instructors act as guides.

## *Personal Development of Higher Education Teachers*

In discussing possible ways through which instructional procedures might be changed, I have concentrated on the rather conventional methods being practised in many higher education institutions. Such approaches may improve the knowledge and skills of teachers but relatively little attention is paid to an issue raised in earlier chapters, that the good teacher is he who is able to use himself effectively, who makes use of his personal qualities to help students learn. If, as I believe, the personal element is so important it would be helpful to set up opportunities for university and college teachers to learn more about themselves as people, how they function, how they "come-across" to other people. One means of creating an environment in which this type of learning becomes possible is the experiential group.

The experiential group normally comprises 7-15 members who meet in an unstructured setting in order to examine their interpersonal relationships. The group itself becomes the focus of enquiry, relying almost exclusively on the behaviour generated by its members. Through the study of such behaviour, participants attempt to understand the dynamics of group processes such as decision making, leadership, norms, roles, communication distortions. The withdrawal of the expected directive leadership and agenda at the beginning of the group experience and the emphasis upon the here-and-now maximizes participants' feelings of responsibility for their own learning. That is, it is primarily *their* behaviour that they explore. It is *their* behaviour that defines the goal. It is *their* responsibility to choose whatever they will learn from the situation, and, if so, how, and how much.

The aim of such an experience is to encourage people to be more aware of the feelings and behaviour of themselves and others. Personal growth is the real goal, hopefully achieved through becoming aware of one's style of personal interaction and discovering more effective ways of being present to others. Interpersonal effectiveness, defined as the degree to which the consequences of one's behaviour match one's intentions, is a key issue. Basically, interpersonal effectiveness would seem to depend upon the ability to communicate precisely what one wants to communicate, to create the impression which one wishes to, to influence the other person in the way one intends. Experience in groups, then, is an attempt to help the individual perceive more clearly his own mode of interaction and to analyze how effective it is. Of far less concern is that participants learn a body of subject matter that has been developed by someone else.

Such a group is usually less concerned with the inner reasons for *why* someone does something, and more concerned with *how* he does it, *what* the impact is on others, and *how* he can improve what he does to become more skilful. This he does by the analysis of here-and-now experiences when the group takes time out from *what* is being discussed to focus on *how* it is being discussed. Under such conditions, participants receive feedback from others, bringing to their attention aspects of their own functioning of which they were unaware.

The expression of feedback is one method by which the experiential group hopes to achieve its aims. A person who interacts gives out information about himself to the group. Other members interpret and comment on this, thus conveying information about his personal style of communication. McLeish, et al., (1973), has pointed out that:

"Within an educational institution, there is little opportunity for this cybernetic process of performance and feedback in relation to personal style of communication. The feedback an individual normally receives in this setting relates only to his intellectual performance, or to a particular skill. But this is just one aspect, perhaps a minor aspect of an overall, personal performance. Education is often directed to the head instead of the whole person. Education frequently has little experiential emphasis."

Feedback is vital to the success of experiential groups. So too is self-disclosure. Participants are expected to talk about themselves in such a way that something of their inner person is conveyed to the other group members. Emphasis is upon here-and-now honesty to reveal what is going on inside one's self with respect to the group interaction. If one feels angry one is expected to say so and to explore, with the help of other participants, the reasons for this anger. Thus the expression of feelings is encouraged. It's really a cyclic process: the effectiveness of one's behaviour depends in large part upon receiving feedback from other individuals; the quality of the feedback one receives from other persons depends largely upon how much one self-discloses (Johnson, 1972).

Clarity of communication, then, would be extremely important in an experiential group, for the receiver must be able to interpret the sender's message in the same way the sender intended it to be interpreted. If this does not occur — the sender misinterprets the sender's message — basic misunderstanding is likely to undermine the interpersonal relationship being developed. Accordingly, listening is a skill emphasized in the group, and this means listening to people rather than to ideas, and attempting to pick up all the cues that others emit, both verbal and non-verbal.

In addition to this accurate communication of feelings to other members, it is important for the participant that he tests perception of the way other people are feeling. This is because the perception of the other person's feelings is more often the result of what you are feeling, or are afraid of, or are wishing for, than of the other person's verbal, non-verbal and behavioural cues (Johnson, 1972). In checking perceptions, the participant states what he perceives to be the feeling of the other person without expressing approval or disapproval of this. Hopefully, the other person will then clarify his own feelings to permit the perception check.

Groups of this type can help an individual to understand himself better and, particularly, to become more perceptive about how other people react to him. This is important for a teacher, who, by the very nature of his task, is constantly in an interpersonal relationship with his students, attempting to communicate with them clearly and unambiguously.

Experience in these groups can be valuable. It can also be useless, and even damaging. Most things we do are like that. Anything worthwhile, that helps us develop our human potentialities involves risk, but facing such situations is a part of growth. Objections can be raised to the use of experiential groups as a means of improving teachers through increasing their self-understanding, but, as Ben Johnson put it: "If all possible objections must first be overcome, nothing would ever be attempted."

A variant on this basic experiential group approach which I have found extremely valuable is the "self-enhancement group" (Stanton, 1978b), the aim of which is to help people to think of themselves in more positive ways. I feel that improving the concept people hold about themselves is possibly the most valuable thing a parent, teacher, or friend can do for another person. Therefore, I have shaped my group work towards this particular end. Combs et al. (1971), have claimed the self-concept to be the chief motivator of behaviour, and that the person who views himself in positive ways is likely to cope with life more successfully than the person who views himself in essentially negative ways. Success seems to breed success and the person who faces life with the expectation of doing things well is likely to have his expectation confirmed. This is just as true of a teacher as it is of anyone else. Through involvement in the self-enhancement group, tertiary teachers may come to develop a more postive self-concept. By so doing, they are likely to become more successful teachers, helping students improve their own self-concepts. I have no hard experimental data to confirm this view, though evidence at the primary and secondary school level does offer some support (Combs et al. 1971). Anecdotal feedback has been highly favourable. This is encouraging. If a person feels he is more confident, and thinks of himself more positively, believing he is likely to be successful in the things he attempts, this is important data for he is the only source of such information. More objective measures, such as increased scores on the Tennessee Self-Concept Scale have confirmed these subjective impressions (Stanton, 1978c), suggesting that the self-enhancement group is achieving its purpose.

Confidence building does seem to be a legitimate concern of a Staff Development Centre, particularly in the light of King's (1973) findings that anxiety about teaching was prevalant among the staff of English universities. She concluded that: ". . . at least at the beginning of a university teacher's career, the emphasis should be put on helping ease anxieties." Ellis & Jones (1974), elaborated upon King's study, concentrating upon lecturing-induced anxiety, and providing considerable evidence that such anxiety leads to very undesirable teaching practices. Helping lecturers to overcome their anxieties through developing a greater sense of self-confidence has been suggested as one way of improving this situation (Harding & Sayer, 1975). This is particularly so for those new to the higher education environment. The self-enhancement group is one way of translating this suggestion into practice. Another is to use positive suggestion, a technique employed in therapeutic situations (Stanton, 1975c, 1977b). If it can be accepted that helping staff members become more self-confident is an appropriate function of a Centre established to improve the standard of teaching and learning in a tertiary institution, it may also be possible to accept the view that some of the Centre's work is likely to be therapeutic in nature. If tertiary teachers do not learn to cope effectively with their anxieties and problems, they are unlikely to improve their teaching to any marked extent, and assisting them to do this could easily be construed as therapy. Experiments (Stanton, 1978c), have been conducted with teacher-trainees and tertiary teachers using positive suggestions and relaxation techniques. These have produced favourable results. Not one subject experienced a decrease in confidence as a result of the experimental treatment whereas 36 out of a total of 48 subjects reported definite gains. The technique used is very simple, showing subjects how to let go and relax so that they would be able to accept positive confidence building suggestions without resistance.

I believe teaching can be improved most effectively through helping lecturers develop their potentialities as human beings. Building self-confidence is part of such development for, as Alexandre Dumas has observed: "A person who doubts himself is like a man who would enlist in the ranks of his enemy and bear arms against himself. He makes failure certain by himself being the first person to be convinced of it". Helping teachers to lose this self-doubt and replace it with self-confidence may be one path to improving higher education. The instructor requires knowledge, presentation skill and these personal qualities which enable him to enthuse and interest his students in the subjects he teaches. Anything that serves to enhance the teacher as a person should help him teach more effectively. The path to improvement of higher education may not lie only with instructional methods, it may also lie with personal enhancement of the people who do the teaching.

# References

ARONSON, E. *The social animal.* San Francisco; W. H. Freeman, 1972.

ABERCROMBIE, M. L. J. The work of a university education research unit. *Universities Quarterly.* 1968. .22. 182-195.

ABERCROMBIE, M. L. J. *The anatomy of judgement.* Penguin, 1969.

ABERCROMBIE, M. L. J. *Aims and techniques of group teaching.* Society for Research into Higher Education. Monograph 12, 1970.

ADELSON, M. On changing higher education from within. *American Behavioural Scientist.* 1974.18.232-249.

AGER, M., & WELTMAN, J. The present structure of university examinations. *Universities Quarterly.* 1967.21.272-285.

ALEXANDER, L. T., GUR, R., & PATTERSON, L. Peer-assisted learning. *Improving Human Performance Quarterly.* 1974. 3. 175-186.

ARGYLE, M. *The psychology of interpersonal behaviour.* Penguin, 1967.

ASCH, M. J. Non-directive teaching in psychology. *Psychology Monographs.* 1951. 65. 4 (whole 321).

ATKIN, J. M. Behavioural objectives in curriculum design: A cautionary note. In: Anderson, R. C., et.al. (Eds.) *Current Research on Instruction.* Englewood & Cliffs, N. J.: Prentice-Hall, 1969. pp.60-65.

AUSTIN, A. W., & LEE, C. B. T. Current practices in the evaluation and training of college teachers. *The Educational Record.* 1966. 47. 361-365.

AUSUBEL, D. *Educational Psychology: A cognitive view.* New York: Holt, Rinehart & Winston, 1968.

BEARD, R. *Teaching and learning in higher eduction.* Penguin, 1970.

BEARD, R. M. & BLIGH, D. A. *Research into teaching methods in higher education.* 3rd edition. Society for Research into Higher Education, 1971.

BIEHLER, R. F. *Psychology applied to teaching.* Boston. Houghton Mifflin. 1971.

BLIGH, D. A. *What's the use of lectures?* Penguin, 1972.

BLOOM, B. *Twenty-five years of educational research. American Education Research Journal.* 1966. 3. 211-221.

BRESLER, J. B. Teaching effectiveness and government awards. *Science.* 1968. 160. 164-167.

BREWER, I. M. Simig: A case study of an innovative method of teaching and learning. *Studies in Higher Education.* 1977.2.33-54.

BROUDY, H. *Three modes of teaching and their evaluation.* Paper presented at APS Conference, Seattle, 1974.

BROWN, E. W., & HENDERSON, R. W. Sharing your inner life with those about you. In: R. W. Henderson (Ed.) *Helping yourself with applied psychology.* Hollywood, California: Wilshire, 1972.

BROWN, G. I. *Human teaching for human learning.* New York: Viking Press, 1971.

BROWN, J. W., LEWIS, R. B., & HARCLEROAD, F. F. *A.V. Instruction — Technology, Media and Methods.* 5th Edition, New York: McGraw-Hill, 1977.

BUGELSKI, B. R. Practical applications of Mower's theory. In: H. F. Clarizio, R. C. Craig & W. A. Mehrens (Eds.). *Contemporary Issues in Educational Psychology.* Boston; Allyn & Bacon, 1970. pp.190-198.

BULL, G. M. An examination of the final examination in medicine. Lancet, 1956. 2. 368-372.

CAPLOW, T., & McGEE, R. J. *The academic marketplace.* New York: Science Editions, 1961.

CAVANAGH, P., & JONES, C. (Eds.) *Yearbook of educational and instructional technology. 1969-70 incorporating programmes in print.* Cornmarket Press, 1969.

CENTRA, J. A. *Strategies for improving college teaching.* Report B. Eric Clearinghouse on Higher Education. Washington, D.C., December, 1972.

CHILDS, G. B. Can we really teach well by correspondence. *National Association of secondary school principals.* 1952. Bulletin 36.

CHISOLM, M. Student evaluation: The red herring of the decade. *Journal of chemical education.* 1977.54.22-3.

CHRISTOPHERSON, D. G. *The engineer in the university.* London: EUP, 1967.

COBURN, T. C. Media and public school communication. In R. A. Weisgerber (Ed). *Instructional process and media innovation.* Chicago: Rand McNally, 1968.

COMBS, A. W. The personal approach to good teaching. *Educational leadership.* 1964.21.369-378.

COMBS, A. W., AVILA, D. L., & PURKEY, W. W. *Helping relationships.* Boston: Allyn & Bacon, 1971.

COMBS, A. W., BLUME, R. A., NEWMAN, A. J., & WASS, H. L. *The professional education of teachers.* 2nd Edition, Boston: Allyn & Bacon, 1974.

COPPEN, H. *Aids to teaching and learning.* Oxford: Pergamon, 1969.

COREY, S. M. quoted by O. Tead in *College teaching and college learning.* New Haven: Yale University Press, 1949.

COSTIN, F. Lecturing versus other methods of teaching: A review of research. *British Journal of Educational Technology.* 1972.3.4-31.

COSTIN, F., GREENOUGH, W. T., & MENGES, R. J. Student ratings of college teaching: Reliability, validity and usefulness. *Review of Educational Research.* 1971.4.511-535.

COX, R. Resistence to change in examining. *Universities Quarterly.* 1967a. 21.352-358.

COX, R. Examinations and higher education: A survey of the literature. *Universities Quarterly.* 1967b. 21.292-340.

CREAGER, J. G., & MURRAY, D. L. (Eds.) *The use of modules in college biology teaching.* Washington: Commission on Undergraduate Education in the Biological Sciences, The American Institute of Biological Science, 1971.

CRONBACH, L. J. How can instruction be adapted to individual differences? in Gagne, R. M. (ed.) *Learning and individual differences.* Columbus, Ohio: Chas. E. Merrill, 1967. pp.23-43.

CROWDER, N. A. On the differences between linear and intrinsic programming. In: J. P. DeCecco (Ed.). *Educational Technology.* New York: Holt, Rinehart & Winston, 1964.

DALE, R. R. University standards. *Universities Quarterly.* 1959.13.186-195.

DAVIS, R. H., ALEXANDER, L. T., & YELON, S. L. *Learning System Design.* New York: McGraw-Hill, 1974.

DAVIS, R. J. Secrets of master lecturers. *Improving College and university teaching.* 1965. 13. 150-151.

DeBLOOIS, M., & ADLER D. D. Stimulating faculty readiness for instructional development: A conservative approach to improving college teaching. *Educational Technology.* 1973. 13. 16-22.

DELECQ, A. L., & Van De VEN, A. H. A group process model for problem identification and program planning. *Journal of Applied Behavioural Science.* 1971.7.466-493.

DIMOCK, H. G. *Planning group development.* Montreal: Sir George Williams University, 1970.

DRUCKNER, A. J., & REMMERS, H. H. Do alumni and students differ in their attitudes towards instructors? *Journal of Educational Psychology.* 1951. 42. 129-143.

DUBERMAN, M. An experiment in education. *Daedalus.* 1968. 97. 318-341.

DUBIN, R., & TAVEGGIA, T. C. *The teaching-learning paradox: A comparative analysis of college teaching methods.* Centre for Advanced Study of Educ Admin: University of Oregon: Oregon, 1968.

DYSINGER, D. W. Performance of correspondence-study students. *Journal of Higher Education, 1957. 28. 387-388.*

EBEL, R. L. Using examinations to promote learning. In: R. M. Cooper (Ed.). *The two ends of the log.* Minneapolis: University of Minnesota Press. 1958. pp.52-63.

EBEL, R. L. Are important objectives testable. In: Page (ed.): *Readings for Educational Psychology.* 1964. pp.132-135.

EISNER, E. W. Educational objectives: Help or hindrance? *The School Review.* 1967.75.250-260.

ELLIS, H. R. & JONES, A. D. Anxiety about lecturing. *Universities Quarterly.* 1974.29.91-95.

ELTON, L. B. R. *Aims and objectives in the teaching of mathematics to non-mathematicians.* Paper presented at Conference on Mathematics for students of other subjects. University of Lancaster, 1970.

ERAUT, M. Promoting innovation in teaching and learning: problems, processes and institutional mechanisms. *Higher Education.* 1975.4.13-26.

FALK, B., & LEE DOW, K. *The assessment of university teaching.* London: Society for Research into Higher Education, 1971.

FAW, F. D. A psychotherapeutic method of teaching psychology. *American Psychologist.* 1949.4.104-109.

FERGUSON, J. *The Open University from within.* London: University of London Press, 1975.

FINCHER, C. The art of teaching. In: S. Lehrer (ed.). *Leaders, teachers and learners in academe.* New York: Appleton-Century-Crofts, 1970.p.418.

FITZGERALD, P. J. The lecture. An arts view. In: Layton, D. (ed.). *University teaching in transition.* Edinburgh: Oliver & Boyd, 1968. pp.11-17.

FLOOD-PAGE, C. The biggest stumbling block in university education. *Universities Quarterly.* 1970.24.266-272.

FLOOD-PAGE, C. Teaching and research — happy symbiosis or hidden warfare? *Universities Quarterly.* 1972.27.102-118.

FLOOD-PAGE, C. *Student evaluation of teaching: The American experience.* London: Society for Research into Higher Education, 1974.

FLOOD-PAGE, C. Teasing hamsters in electric cages. *Universities Quarterly.* 1975-29.3.318-331.

FLOOD-PAGE, C. *Technical aids to teaching in higher education.* 2nd.Ed. Society for Research into Higher Education, 1976.

FREYBERG, P. S. The effectiveness of note-taking. *Education for Teaching.* 1956 (Feb.) 17-24.

FUREDY, C. Centres for improving university teaching: Australian approaches. *Ontario Universities Program for Instructional Development. Newsletter,* 1975.5.2-4.

GADZELLA, B. College students' views and ratings of an ideal professor. *College & University.* 1968.44.89-96.

GAFF, J. G. Making a difference: the impacts of faculty. *Journal of Higher Education.* 1973.44.605-622.

GAGE, N. L., RUNKEL, P. J., & CHATTERJEE, B. B. Changing teacher behaviour through feedback from pupils: An application of equilibrium theory. In: Charters, W. W. Jr., & Gage, N. L. (Eds.). *Readings in the Social Psychology of Education.* Boston: Allyn & Bacon, 1963. pp.173-180.

GARTNER, A., KOHLER, M., & PRESSMAN, F. *Children teach children: Learning by teaching.* New York: Harper & Row, 1971.

GERLACH, V. S. & ELY, D. P. *Teaching and media: A systematic approach.* Englewood Cliffs, N.J., Prentice-Hall, 1971.

GILBERT, T. F. Mathetics: The technology of education. *Journal of Mathetics.* 1962.1.7-73.

GILBRAN, K. *The prophet.* Heinemann; London, 1926.

GOLDBERG, L. R. Student personality characteristics and optional college learning conditions: An extensive search for trait-by-trait interaction effects. *Instructional Science.* 1972.1.153-210.

GOLDMAN, R. M., WADE, S., & ZEGAR, D. Students without harness: The 'sum' experiment in self-paced learning. *Journal of Higher Education.* 1974.45.197-210.

GOLDSCHMID, B., & GOLDSCHMID, M. L. Individualizing instruction in higher education: A review. *Higher Education.* 1973.3.1-24.

GOLDSCHMID, M. L. Instructional options: Adapting the large university course to individual differences. *Learning & Development.* 1970.1.1-2.

GOLDSCHMID, M. L. The learning cell: An instructional innovation. *Learning & Development.* 1971.2.1-6.

GOLDSCHMID, M. L., & SHORE, B. M. The learning cell: A field test of an educational innovation. In: W. A. Verreck (Ed.). *Methodological problems in research and development in higher education.* Amsterdam: Swets & Zeitlinger, B. C., 1974. pp.218-236.

GOOD, T. L., BIDDLE, B. J., & BROPHY, J. E. *Teachers make a difference.* New York: Holt, Rinehart & Winston, 1975.

GOODE, D. M. All that they most revered. In: H. A. Estrin & D. M.Goode (Eds.). *College & University Teaching.* Iowa: Wm. C. Brown, 1964. pp.34-35.

GREEN, B. A. Physics teaching by the Keller Plan at MIT. *American Journal of Physics.* 1971.39.764-775.

GRONLUND, N. E. *Constructing achievement tests.* Englewood Cliffs, N.J.: Prentice-Hall, 1968.

GRUBER, H. M. The uses and abuses of negative results. In: O. Milton & E. J.Shohen Jnr. (Eds.). *Learning and the professors.* Ohio: Ohio University Press, 1968.

GUTHRIE, E. R. *The evaluation of teaching: A progress report.* Seattle: University of Washington, 1954.

HAEFELE, D. L. Self-instruction and teacher education. *Audiovisual instruction.* Jan.1969.14.1., 63-64.

HALL, W. C. *Evaluating courses.* Advisory Centre for University Education, University of Adelaide, 1977a.

HALL, W. C. Models for tertiary teaching units. *Australian Journal of Education.* 1977b.21.55.64.

HALL, W. C. Teaching in higher education. In D. Unwin & R. McAleese (Eds.). *Encyclopedia of Educational Technology.* London: McMillan, 1977c.

HALL, W. C., & CANNON, R. *University teaching.* Advisory Centre for University Education. The University of Adelaide. South Australia, 1975.

HAMMOND, P. E., MEYER, J. W., & MILLER, D. Teaching versus research: Sources of misperceptions. *Journal of Higher Education.* 1969.40.682-690.

HARDING, A.G., & SAYER, S. The objectives of training university teachers. *Universities Quarterly.* 1975.29.299-317.

HARTLEY, J. & MARSHALL, S. On notes and note-taking. *Universities Quarterly.* 1974.28.225-235.

HARTLEY, J. & CAMERON, A. Some observations on the efficiency of lecturing. *Educational Review.* 1967.20.30-37.

HENDERSHOT, C. H. *Programmed learning: A bibliography of programs and presentation devices.* 4th Ed. Bay City, Michigan: Carl H. Hendershot, with supplements to 1971. 1967.

HENDERSON, N. K. *University teaching.* Hong Kong University Press, 1969.

HIGHETT, G. *The art of teaching.* London: Methuen, 1951.

HILDERBRAND, M. How to recommend promotion for a mediocre teacher without actually lying. *Journal of Higher Education.* 1972.43.44-62.

HILDERBRAND, M., & WILSON, R. C. *Effective university teaching and its evaluation.* Berkeley, California: Centre for Research & Development in Higher Education, 1970.

HILDERBRAND, M., WILSON, R. C., & DIENST, E. R. *Evaluating university teaching.* Berkeley, California: Centre for Research & Development in Higher Education, 1971.

HIMMELWEIT, H. T. Towards a rationalization of examination procedures. *Universities Quarterly,* 1967.21.359-372.

HOLT, J. *How children fail.* Penguin, 1960.

HOLT, J. *How children learn.* London; Pitman & Sons, 1967.

HOWE, H. Less teaching, more conversation. In: C. B. T. Lee (ed.). *Improving College Teaching.* Washington, D.C.: American Council in Education, 1967. pp.259-264.

HOYT, D. P. The relationship between college grades and adult achievement. *A.C.T. Research Report No.7.* American College Testing Programme: Iowa, September, 1965.

JACOB, P. *Changing values in college.* New York: Harper, 1957.

JOHNSON, D. W. *Reaching out.* Englewood Cliffs. N. J.: Prentice-Hall, 1972.

JOHNSON, J. A. Instruction: From the consumer's view. In: C. B. T. Lee (Ed.). *Improving College Teaching.* Washington, D.C.: American Council on Education, 1967.288-292.

KAPFER, M. B., & DELLA-PIANA, G. M. Educational technology in the in-service education of university teaching fellows. *Educational Technology.* 1974.14.22-28.

KELLER, F. S. Engineering personalized instruction in the classroom. *Rev.Interamer. de Psicol.* 1967.1.189-197.

KELLER, F. S. Good-bye teacher. *J. App. Behav. Analy.* 1968.1.79-89.

KENT, L. Student evaluation of teaching. In: C. B. T. Lee (Ed.). *Improving College Teaching.* Washington, D.C.: American Council on Education, 1967. pp.312-343.

KILBY, J. E. Group dynamics and college english. *J. English Teaching Techniques.* 1974.7.38-45.

KING, M. The anxieties of university teachers. *Universities Quarterly.* 1973.28.69-83.

KLEMM, W. R. Efficiency of handout 'skeleton' notes in student learning. *Improving College & University Teaching.* 1976.24.10-12.

LAING, A. The art of lecturing: In: Layton, D.(Ed.). *University teaching in transition*.p.18-33. Edinburgh: Olives & Boyd, 1968.

LANE, M. Clustering. *Improving College & University Teaching*. 1975.23.203-206.

LANGEN, T. F. D. Student assessment of teaching effectiveness. *Improving College & University Teaching*. 1966.14.22-25.

LEHMANN, R. Evaluation of instruction. In: P. Dressel, et.al. (Eds.) *Evaluations in Higher Education*. Office of Institutional Research, Boston: Houghton Mifflin, 1961.

LITTLE, G. *The university experience*. Melbourne: Melbourne University Press, 1970.

LLOYD, D. H. A concept of improvement of learning response in the taught lesson. *Visual Education*. October, 1968.

LONDON, Perry. Kidding around with hypnosis. *Int. J. Clin. & Exp. Hypnosis*. 1976. 24. 105-121.

MACE, C. A. *The psychology of study*. London: Methuen, 1932.

MADDOX, H. *How to study*. London: Pan Books, 1963.

MAGER, R. F. On the sequencing of instructional content. *Psychology Reports*. 1961. 9. 405-413.

MAGER, R. F. *Preparing instructional objectives*. San Francisco, California: Fearon. 1961.

MAGER, R. F. *Developing attitude toward learning*. Palo Alto, California: Fearon. 1968.

MAGER, R. F., & CLARK, 1969. Explorations in student controlled instruction. in R. C. Anderson et. al. (Eds.) *Current research in Education*. Englewood Cliffs, N. J., Prentice Hall, 1969. pp. 54-59.

MAIER, N. R. F. *Problem-solving discussions and conferences: Leadership method and skills*. New York: McGraw-Hill, 1963.

MARSHALL, Peter. How much, how often? *College & Research Libraries*. 1974. 34. 6. 453-6.

MILLER, A. H. The preparation of tertiary teachers. *The Australian University*. 1976. 14. 33-42.

MILLER, R. I. *Evaluation faculty performance*. San Francisco: Jossey-Bass, 1972.

MILTON, O. *Alternatives to the traditional*. San Francisco: Jossey-Bass, 1973.

MOODY, A., & BAUSELL, R. *The effect of relevant teaching practice in the elicitation of student achievement*. Paper presented at annual meeting of American Educational Research Association; New Orleans, 1973.

MOUNTFORD, J. *British Universities*. O.U.P. 1966.

MUELLER, R. H., ROACH, P. J., & MALONE, J. A. College students views of the characteristics of an "ideal" professor. *Psychology in the schools*. 1971. 8. 161-166.

MACKIE, R. R., & CHRISTENSEN, P. R. *Translation & application of psychological research*. Goleta, California: Human Factors Research Inc., 1967.

McDONALD, R. L., & DODGE, R. A. Audio-tutorial packages at Columbia Junior College. In: J. G. Graeger & D. L. Murray (Eds.). *The use of modules in college biology teaching*. Washington, D.C.: Commission on Undergraduate Education in the Biological Sciences, The American Institute of Biological Sciences, 1971. pp. 45-52.

McKEACHIE, W. J. The improvement of instruction. *Rev.Educ.Res*. 1960.30.351-360.

McKEACHIE, W. J. Current research on teaching effectiveness. In: H. A. Estrin & D. M. Goode (Eds.). *College & University Teaching*. Dubuque, Iowa: Wm. C. Brown. 1964. pp.377-386.

McKEACHIE, W. J. *Teaching tips: A guidebook for the beginning college teacher*. 6th Ed., Lexington, Mass.; Heath & Co., 1969a.

McKEACHIE, W. J. Student ratings of faculty. *AAUP Bulletin*. 1969b. 55. 439-444.

McKEACHIE, W. J., & KULIK, J. A. *Effective college teaching*. Inc. F. N. Kerlinger (Eds.) *Review of Research in Education* Peacock, 1975.

MacKENZIE, N., ERAUT, H. & JONES, H. C. *Teaching & learning: An introduction to new methods and resources in higher education*. Paris. UNESCO and The International Association of Universities. 1970.

McLEISH, J., MATHESON, W., & PARK, J. *The psychology of the learning group*. London. Hutchinson. 1973.

MacMANAWAY, L. A. Teaching methods in higher education — innovation and research. *Universities Quarterly*. 1970. 24. 321-329.

McMILLAN, J. H. The impact of instructional improvement agencies in higher education. *Journal of Higher Education*. 1975. 46. 17-23.

NACHMAN, M., & OPOCHINSKY, S. The effects of different teaching methods: A methodological study. *J.Educ.Psych*. 1958. 49. 245-249.

NAPIER, R. W. & GERSHENFIELD, M. K. *Groups: Theory & experience*. Boston. Houghton Mifflin. 1973.

NOLAN, J. D. Are lectures necessary? *Improving College & University Teaching*.1974. 22. 253-256.

NUFFIELD FOUNDATION. *The group for research and innovation in higher education*. London, 1973-75.

NYBERG, D. The coagulation method of starting lecture-discussion courses. *Improving College & University Teaching*. 1976. 24. 35-36.

O'DOWD, D. D. Closing the gap. In: C. B. T. Lee (Ed.) *Improving College Teaching*. Washington, D.C., American Council on Education. 1967. pp.248-251.

OETTINGER, A. G.*Run, computor, run: The Mythology of educational innovation*. Cambridge, Massachusetts: Harvard Univ. Press. 1969.

OTTAWAY, A. K. G. Teaching small groups. In: D. Layton (Ed.) *University teaching in transition*. Edinburgh. Oliver & Boyd, 1968. pp.53-62.

PIAGET, J. & INHELDER, B. *The psychology of the child*. New York: Basic Books, 1969.

PIERON, H. *Examins & docimologie*. Paris: P.U.F., 1963.

POPHAM, W. Teaching skill under scrutiny. *Phi Delta Kappan*. 1971.52.599-602.

POSTLETHWAIT, S. N. & RUSSELL, J. D. "Minicourses" — the style of the future. In: J. G. Creager & D. L. Murray (Eds.). *The uses of modules in college biology teaching.* Washington, D.C.: Commission on Undergraduate Education in the Biological Sciences, the American Institute of Biological Sciences, 1971. pp.19-29.

POSTMAN, W. & WEINGARTNER, G. *Teaching as a subversive activity.* Penguin, 1971.

POTTS, D. *Discussion methods for learning. Self & Society.* 1975.3.1-12.

POWELL, L. S. *Lecturing.* Pitman, 1973.

PRESSEY, S. L. Teaching machine (and learning theory) crisis. *Journal of Applied Psychology.* 1963. 47. 1-6.

RAUSHENBUSH, E. Innovation and educational style. In: C. T. B. Lee (Ed.). *Improving College Teaching.* Washington, D.C., American Council on Education, 1967. pp.197-201.

REMMERS, H. H. Rating methods in research on teaching. In: N. L. Gage (Ed.). *Handbook of Research on Teaching.* Chicago; Rand McNally, 1963.

REMMERS, H. H., & WEISBRODT, J. A. *Manual of instructions for the purdue ratings scale for instruction.* West Lafayette Indiana University Book Store, 1965.

REZLER, A. G., & ANDERSON, A. S. Focussed and unfocussed feedback and self-perception. *Journal of Educational Research.* 1971. 65. 61-64.

ROBINSON, F. P. *Effective Study.* New York: Harper & Bros., 1946.

ROCKART, J. F. A method for the integrated use of learning resources in education. Journal of Higher Education. 1973. 44. 281-298.

ROE, E. *Using and misusing the materials of teaching and learning: Studies in efficiency of communication in higher education.* Canberra Education Research Unit, Research School of Social Sciences, Aust. National University, 1975.

ROGERS, C. *Freedom to learn. Columbus, Ohio; Chas. E. Merrill, 1969.*

ROWNTREE, D. *Learn how to study:* London, McDonald, 1970.

ROWNTREE, D. *Educational technology in curriculum development.* London: Harper & Row, 1974.

ROID, G. H. Towards a system of course evaluation. *Learning and development.* 1971. 2. 1-5.

RYANS, D. G. Research on teacher behaviour in the context of the teacher characteristics study. In: B. J. Biddle & W. J. Ellena. (Eds.). *Contemporary Research on Teacher Effectiveness.* New York: Holt, Rinehart & Winston, 1964, pp.67-101.

SANFORD, N. Academic culture and the teacher's development. *Soundings.* Winter, 1971.

SAUNDERS, M. University teaching — A student point of view. In: D. Layton (Ed.) *University Teaching in Transition.* Edinburgh: Oliver & Boyd, 1968. pp. 149-161.

SCHONELL, F. J., ROE, E., & MIDDLETON, I. G. *Promise & performance.* The University of Queensland Press, 1962.

SHANNON, R. L. *Where the truth comes out: humanistic education.* Columbus, Ohio. Merrill, 1971.

SHEEHAN, D. S. The localization, diagnostic, and monitoring functions of student ratings in a model for improving university teaching. *Instructional Science.* 1976. 5. 77-92.

SHEFFIELD, E. F. (Ed.) *Teaching in the universities.* Montreal: McGill-Queen's University Press, 1974.

SHERMAN, J. G. (Ed.). *Personalized system of instruction newsletter.* Washington, D. C., Psychology Department, Georgetown University. 1971, 1972.

SILBERMAN, M. L. & ALLENDER, I. S. The course description: A semiprojective technique for assessing students' reactions to college classes. *Journal of Higher Education.* 1974. 45. 450-457.

SKINNER, B. F. Teaching machines. *Science.* 1958. 128. 91-102.

SKINNER, B. F. *The technology of teaching.* New York: Appleton-Century-Crofts, 1968.

SLOBIN, D. Y., & NICHOLS, D. G. Student rating of teaching. *Improving College & University Teaching.* 1969. 17. 244-248.

SMYTHE, A. B. Free discussion groups for Biology I students. *The Australian University.* 1974.12. 147-165.

SNYGG, D. A. Cognitive-field theory of learning. In: D. L. Avila, A. W. Combs & W. W. Purkey (Eds.). *The helping relationship sourcebook.* Boston: Allyn & Bacon, 1972.

STANTON, H. E. Evaluating the effective objectives of education. *Vestes.* 1970.13. 265-271.

STANTON, H. E. A diagnostic rating of teacher performance scale. *Australian Journal of Education.* 1971. 15. 95-103.

STANTON, H. E. The 'ideal' lecturer as seen by the Australian student. *The Australian University.* 1972a. 10. 15-20.

STANTON, H. E. Rating or inventory: A comparison of two approaches to personality measurement. *Australian Psychologist.* 1972b. 7. 33-39.

STANTON, H. E. The interaction of tertiary teaching methods with student personality. Unpublished doctoral dissertation. Flinders University of South Australia. 1972c.

STANTON, H. E. Measurable objectives. In: W. S. Simpkins & A. H. Miller (Eds.). *Changing Education.* New York: McGraw-Hill, 1972d. pp. 74-80.

STANTON, H. E. Teacher education and the 'good' teacher. *The Educational Forum.* 1973. Vol. 37. 25-30.

STANTON, H. E. Teaching methods and student personality — the search for an elusive interaction. *Instructional Science.* 1974a. 2. 477-502.

STANTON, H. E. Improving university teaching. *The Australian University.* 1974b. 12. 264-269.

STANTON, H. E. Facilitating learning — a humanistic approach to the 'teaching' of educational psychology. *Australian Psychologist.* 1975a. 10. 50-58.

STANTON, H. E. Do university students want to learn. *The Australian University.* 1975b. 13. 160-164.

113

STANTON, H. E. Ego-enhancement through positive suggestion. *Australian Journal of Clinical Hypnosis.* 1975c. 2. 32-36.

STANTON, H. E. Teacher education and the experiential group. *Contemporary Educational Psychology.* 1976. 1. 89-97.

STANTON, H. E. Dyadic discussion as a teaching method. *Contemporary Educational Psychology.* 1977a. 2. 99-107.

STANTON, H. E. The utilization of suggestions derived from rational-emotive therapy. *International Journal of Clinical & Experimental Hypnosis.* 1977b. 25. No 1, 18-26.

STANTON, H. E. Self-grading as an assessment method. *Improving College and University Teaching.* 1978a (in press).

STANTON, H. E. The self-enhancement group: Helping people to like themselves. *Wholistic education: The Journal of Humanistic and Transpersonal Education.* 1978b (in press).

STANTON, H. E. Improving lecturer performance through confidence building. *S.A.L.T. Journal.* 1978c (in press).

STATON, T. *R.S.V.P. A dynamic approach to study.* Glenview, Illinois: Scott Foresman, 1966.

STEPHENS, J. M. *The process of schooling.* New York: Holt, Rinehart & Winston, 1967.

STEWART, D. *Educational Malpractices.* California: Slate Services, 1971.

TERC. *Evaluation of teaching.* Occasional Publication 6. Tertiary Education Research Centre, University of New South Wales, September, 1976.

THIAGARAJAN, S. Madras system revisited: A new structure for peer tutoring. *Educational Technology.* 1973. 13. 10-13.

TOSTI, D. T. The peer proctor in individualized programs. *Educational Technology.* 1973. 13. 29-30.

TYLER, R. W. The evaluation of teaching. In: D. A. Albright & J. E. Barrows (Eds.). *Preparing College Teachers.* Lexington, Kentucky: University of Kentucky, 1959.

UNIVERSITY GRANTS COMMITTEE. *Reports of the Committee on University Teaching Methods.* (Chairman: Sir E. Hale), HMSA. 1964.

UNWIN, D. (Ed.). *Media & methods: Instructional technology in higher education.* McGraw-Hill, 1969.

UTMU. *Improving teaching in higher education.* University of London Teaching Methods Unit, 1976.

VAN DER BERGHE, P. *Academic gamesmanship.* London: Abelard-Schuman, 1970.

VAN DER KLAUW, C. F., & PLOMP, T. Individualized study systems in theory and practice. *Higher Education.* 1974. 3. 213-230.

VOEKS, V. W. Publications and teaching effectiveness. *Journal of Higher Education.* 1962. 33. 212.218.

WARE, J. E., & WILLIAMS, R. G. The Dr. Fox effect: A study of lecturer effectiveness and ratings of instruction. *J. Medical Education.* 1975. 50. 149-156.

WELSMAN, R. A. & SHAPIRO, D. M. Personalized system of instruction (Keller method) for medical school biochemistry. *Journal of Medical Education.* 1973. 48. 934-938.

WHITEHURST, C. & MADIGAN, J. Slow learners in PSI courses: Do they learn less? *J. Higher Education.* 1975. 46. 55-62.

WIGHT, A. R. Beyond behavioural objectives. *Educational Technology.* 1972. 12. 9-14.

WILHELMS, F. T. Actualizing the effective professional worker in education. In: Bower & Hollister (Eds.). *Behavioural Science Frontiers in Education.* Wiley, 1967. pp. 357-378.

WISPE, L. G. Evaluating section teaching methods in the introductory course. *Journal of Educational Research.* 1951. 45. 161-186.

WITTICH, W. A., & SCHULLER, C. F. *Instructional technology — its nature and use.* New York: Harper & Row, 1973.

# Index

academics,
  teaching role 2, 16-17, 98-9
  research role 2-3, 98
assessment, 83-4
  by continuous assessment 96
  by essays 96
  by student self-assessment 96
  by testing of mastery 93-4
audiotape 80
audio-visual material *see* media

blackboard 45
  use in group discussion 58
brainstorming 59
buzz groups 42

competition 13
course aims 4, 10, 11-12, 75-6
  achievement of 77-8
  assessment of students in terms of 96-7
course content 8-9, 26
course design 75-6
course evaluation questionnaire 89-90, 90-91
course objectives 78
  *see also* course aims

decision group 47
discussion 23
  in lectures 8, 41, 42-3
  value compared with lecture 27-8
discussion, dyadic 53-6
discussion groups 11, 47-61
  advantages 48-51
  disadvantages 49-51
  leader 48, 57
  in pairs 53-6
  preparation of students for 56-7
  purposes 48-51
  seating 48, 57
  size 47

emotions 11
evaluation 83-4
examinations 6, 7, 26, 30, 95-7
  as measures of teaching effectiveness 27, 28, 83
  purposes of 92-3
experiential groups 105-6
exposition 36

group processes 52-3, 59-61

handouts 43-5
higher education, aims 49

independent study techniques 23, 62-73
  individualized systems 64-73
  modular instruction 66-9
  personalized system 64-6
  programmed instruction 69-71
  for laboratory classes 71-2
inductive teaching 9-10
Instructional Development Centres 90, 100-4

laboratory classes 71-2
learning,
  definition 7
  components 7-8
  from lectures 6-7
learning group 47
lecture 6, 23, 25-6, 29, 34-46
  advantages of 37-8
  aim given in handout 43
  emphasis of key points 45
  faults 34-5
  for information transfer 35-6
  lecture notes as handouts 43-4
  structure 39-41
  for subject criticism 36
  techniques 9-10, 38-9
  value compared with discussion 27-8
lecture-discussion 41-2
lecturer,
  use of notes or full script 46
  personality of 36
  reaction to audience 46
  as a resource 29
listening skills 35-6, 37


mastery, testing of 93-4
meaning, understanding of 8-11
media,
  expert assistance with 102
  incorporation in courses 74, 78-81
  value of 79, 81-2
motivation 10, 11-12


nominal group technique 58-9

Open University 4, 99
  Technological Foundation Course 71

peer teachers 8, 65-6
proctors 65-6

RSVP 14, 16
reading efficiency 13-14
reading, guided 28, 44-5
research 2-3, 98

SQ3R method 13-14
scholar as teacher 16-17
self concept 107-8
self reward 10
seminar 48
  leader 48

Staff Development Centre *see*
Instructional Development Centre
students
  change attitudes of 50
  contribution to education 13
  in discussion groups 47, 57-8, 59-61
    acquaintanceship 56, 59
    interaction 52, 53
  individual responses to different methods 29, 37
  preference for lectures 35
  reward for competence 65
  self-assessment 95
  tutorial preparation 56

tape-slide programmes 80
teachers,
  attitudes to students 19, 20, 21
  characteristics of 1, 16-21
  competence with material 20
  enthusiasm for subject 18, 20, 21
  evaluation by students 84, 85-92
    methods 88-92
    objections 87-88
  evaluation by teacher specialists 101
  good scholar as teacher 20
  interaction with students 23-4, 26, 29
  training 1, 3, 104-5
teaching,
  evaluation of effectiveness by students 85-92
  evaluation of effectiveness by other teachers 84-5
  goals 1
  good 1
  ineffective 4
  research into 3, 24-5, 98
teaching methods 3-4, 9-10
  alternatives within a course 29
  comparison of 26-8
  feedback necessary 35
  innovation 100, 101-2
  obstacles to change 99
  student preference 27-8
teaching styles 22-3
tertiary teacher training 104-5
threat 12-13
tutor 48, 50, 51-2
  skill in group methods 52, 57-8
  questioning technique 57
tutorials 48

Utah State University Learning Resources Program 30-2

visuals 79-80